TO YOU

Zen Sayings of Kōdō Sawaki

TO YOU

Zen Sayings of Kōdō Sawaki

Translated by
Muhō Nöelke and Reihō Jesse Haasch

HOHM PRESS
Chino Valley, Arizona

Cover Design: Hohm Press, Chino Valley, Arizona, 86323

Interior Design and Layout: Becky Fulker, Kubera Book Design, Prescott, Arizona

Library of Congress Control Number: 2021941130

ISBN: 978-1-942493-70-9
e-book: 978-1-942493-71-6

Hohm Press
P.O. Box 4410
Chino Valley, AZ 86323
800-381-2700
http://www.hohmpress.com

This book was printed in the U.S.A. on recycled, acid-free paper using soy ink.
Translated from Japanese: *Kōdō Sawaki: Zen ni kike*, Daihorinkaku, 1986.
ISBN 978-4-804610-80-1

CONTENTS

INTRODUCTION

by Kōshō Uchiyama

Shiojiri, Nagano, mid-summer 1986*

About the Conditions Which Led to Kōdō Sawaki's Greatness

More than twenty years have gone by since the death of Sawaki Rōshi, a leading figure in the world of Zen who was active from the 1920s to 1965. Even today, the immense influence that he has had on our society can be felt. Yet the conditions he was born into were unimaginably difficult and impoverished.

He was born in 1880 in Mie Prefecture. Japan was in the process of reforming itself politically and the new nation still lacked a stable foundation. In those uncertain times, when he was only four years old his mother passed away, and when he was seven he experienced the sudden death of his father. The four brothers and sisters were divided among the families of relatives or became servants. Sawaki Rōshi, who was called Saikichi as a child, went to an uncle's home. This uncle, though, also passed away a half-year later, and he was adopted

---

* This Introduction was written for the first edition, published in Japanese in 1986.

by Bunkichi Sawaki, who officially operated a paper lantern business in the town of Isshinden, but in reality made his money through gambling.

This is where Saikichi spent his four years of primary school. As he started late, he did not finish until he was twelve. The boy worked as an errand boy for his stepparents. He learned about the world of gambling by selling rice cakes in the parlors and keeping an eye on the guest's sandals. Once he witnessed how a fifty-year-old man, who had hired an eighteen-year-old prostitute, died from a heart attack, and how his wife came in the next morning crying, "Even in death he has to make things difficult for me—and in a place like this!"

So Saikichi, as a young boy, had already experienced what happens behind the curtains of our complicated world. Shortly after having finished primary school, a bloody dispute took place between roughly seventy gangsters fighting over the borders of their territories. In the evening, Saikichi's stepfather was faced with the thankless job of establishing contact between groups of fleeing gangsters. Shaking with fear, he was unable to fulfill his mission. In his place, Saikichi volunteered. In the middle of the night, in a terrible rain, he crossed the scene of the bloody battle and reestablished contact between the gangsters who were already ten km. away. From that night on, his stepfather began to fear him and stopped beating him.

Though Sawaki Rōshi spent his childhood years in such a milieu, he also had other role models. There was the Morita family, who were scraping out a living in a rundown backhouse. The father glued calligraphy rolls, while the son studied traditional Japanese painting. Saikichi felt drawn to this family, whose life, although it took place in the most impoverished conditions, had something very pure about it. So he began to come and go at the Morita home.

He studied old Chinese and Japanese history and literature from the father of the Morita family. Moreover, he learned the truth that there are things in life more important than money, position and fame. Later, Sawaki Rōshi himself said that this was how the bud formed, out of which the fruit of his later life ripened.

After finishing primary school, Saikichi took over the paper-lantern business, which was how he fed his hedonistic adoptive parents (his stepmother had been a prostitute). Yet gradually, he was beginning to open his eyes to his own life. He began to wonder if it was right to live his life like that, only to later marry and feed a wife and children. He didn't know up from down, but his mind clearly yearned for the way.

When he ran away for the first time, Saikichi ended up at the home of an acquaintance in Osaka. Yet this escape was unsuccessful: his adoptive parents picked him up again. The next time, he was determined to run so far away that no one would ever be able to catch him again.

As a sixteen-year-old, with three kilos of rice on his shoulders and twenty-seven sen in his pocket, he marched with the light of a single lantern to Eiheiji temple in Echizen, constantly chewing on the raw rice throughout the long journey. Eiheiji could not be bothered with the runaway and Saikichi was refused entry. For two days and two nights he waited without food or water in front of the gate in the hope that his request would be heard: "Please ordain me as a monk or let me die here before the gates of Eiheiji." In the end, he was taken in as an assistant in Eiheiji's workshop. Later, he helped out at Ryūunji, the temple of a leading priest from Eiheiji.

At one point he had a day off and decided to do zazen in his own room. By chance, an old parishioner who helped out at the temple entered the room and bowed towards him respectfully, as if he were the Buddha himself. This old woman usually just ordered him around like an errand boy. So what was it that moved her to bow towards him with such respect? This was the first time that Sawaki Rōshi realized what noble dignity was inherent in the zazen posture, and he resolved to practice zazen for the rest of his life. In his old age, Sawaki Rōshi often said that he was a man who had wasted his entire life with zazen. The point of departure for this way of life lay in this early event.

Due to various circumstances, his wish to become monk was finally granted, and he was ordained in Sōshinji in distant Kyūshū. At the age of nineteen, he entered Entsūji in Tanba as a trainee monk, but only stayed a fortnight. From there, he was sent to another temple in which he met Ryōun Fueoka Rōshi. They understood each other well, and Sawaki resolved to follow him.

Fueoka Rōshi had studied for years under Bokuzan Nishiari Zenji, a great Zen master of the Meiji Era (1868-1912), and the longer they were together, the more Sawaki Rōshi was attracted to his straightforward character. Sawaki Rōshi heard lectures from Fueoka Rōshi on *Gakudōyōjinshū*, *Eiheishingi* and *Zazenyōjinki*, which formed the basis of his later practice of *shikantaza*, just sitting.

Following that, Sawaki was drafted as a soldier in the Japanese-Russian War (which broke out in 1904) and earned a golden medal. At the age of twenty-six, in the year 1906, he returned to Japan. After the war, rather late for his age he entered the Academy for Buddhist Studies in his hometown, after which he transferred to the seminar of Hōryūji in Nara where he studied Yogacara philosophy under the abbot Jōin Saeki Sōjō.

At the age of thirty-four, after having obtained this overview of Buddhist teaching, he began to practice zazen alone from morning until night at Jōfukuji, an empty temple in Nara. Here shikantaza penetrated his flesh and blood. In 1916, when he was thirty-six, Sōtan Oka Rōshi, recruited him as a teacher for the monks in Daijiji in Higo. After Oka Rōshi's death, Sawaki Rōshi lived alone on Mannichi Mountain in Kumamoto, and with this as his base, he began to travel to all parts of Japan to give instruction on zazen and hold lectures.

When he was fifty-five, he was appointed professor at Komazawa University. At the same time, he became *godō* (a head teacher) at Sōjiji, one of the two main temples of the Sōtō school. This began the period of Sawaki Rōshi's greatest activity.

At that time, "Zen" didn't mean much more than the kōan Zen of the Rinzai School, but Sawaki Rōshi concentrated entirely on shikantaza as it had been taught by Dōgen Zenji. Looking at the history of Japanese Buddhism, it cannot be overlooked that Sawaki Rōshi was the first in our era to reintroduce shikantaza in its pure form and revive it as being equally valid as kōan Zen.

Because he never lived in his own temple and also did not write any books, people began to name him "Homeless Kōdō." Yet, in 1963, he lost the strength in his legs and he had to give up traveling. He retired to Antaiji where he died in 1965 at the age of eighty-five.

About This Work

I was ordained as a monk on the eighth of December 1941, the day of the outbreak of the Pacific War between Japan and America. I then followed Sawaki Rōshi for exactly twenty-four years until his death on the twenty-first of December 1965. I have to admit that my teacher was always traveling, but still he spent about a week every month with his attendants in order to practice with us and to preach the dharma.

During these dharma talks, for my own practice, I took notes of sayings that seemed to be especially important expressions of the dharma. With the years, this mountain of notes took on enormous dimensions. As it seemed to me a pity to let these notes go to waste in my private notebooks, I began to publish them in a monthly journal. Many of Sawaki Rōshi's sayings in this book first appeared there. A number of years after his death, a publishing house became interested in a reissue, which was also my wish.

However, my advanced age led me to retire from the task of reorganizing and publishing the huge volume of fragments. So, I gave the work over to my disciple Shūsoku Kushiya, who has now followed me for seventeen years and takes care of me day and night, as I myself had previously taken care of Sawaki Rōshi. Shūsoku was pleased to take on the task and began delving into the sayings of Sawaki Rōshi, the teacher of his own teacher.

In the arrangement of the fragments, the reader will notice Shūsoku's youthful, modern approach. He has sorted the quotations into chapters which all begin with "To you who…" This allows the reader to get an overview of the entire book and to be able to open to the chapter that is most relevant at the moment. In this way, the reader will gradually become interested in other chapters, expanding and deepening step-by-step his understanding of the teaching of Sawaki Rōshi.

I am very satisfied with this approach. Each of the quotations has a fascinating power, which would be wasted if the sayings were simply listed randomly one after the other. The point of focus would be lost. Yet not a single one of these quotations deserves to be quickly read and then forgotten, for they are all about ourselves. Their deeper meaning is only revealed when we take the time to chew over these sayings in peace, digest them, and "see the mind in light of the ancient teachings."

I hope that the words of my teacher will penetrate your flesh and blood and will become a part of yourself, for this book represents the living teaching of Sawaki Rōshi. I hope to have made the warmth of this living teaching tangible by writing down his words.

Furthermore, because my disciple Kushiya as part of his own practice has presented these aphorisms in such a fresh and youthful way, here are now three generations of teachers and students united. Sawaki Rōshi would have been very pleased with this result.[†]

[†] As we hope he would be happy with this English translation, the combined effort of later generations of Western disciples from two Sawaki Rōshi lineages. —Translators

Zen Sayings of Kōdō Sawaki

To you who can't stop worrying about how others see you

You can't even trade a single fart with the next guy.
Each and every one of us has to live out his own life.

The eyes don't say, "Sure we're lower, but we see more."
The eyebrows don't reply, "Sure we don't see anything, but
we *are* higher up."

Living out the buddha-dharma means fulfilling your
function completely without knowing that you're doing it.
A mountain doesn't know it's tall. The sea doesn't know it's
wide and deep. Each and every thing in the universe is active
without knowing it.

*The bird's singing and the flower's laughter appear naturally,
completely independent from the person sitting in zazen at the
foot of the cliff.*

The bird doesn't sing in honor of the person in zazen. The
flower doesn't blossom to amaze the person with her beauty.
In exactly the same way, the person doesn't sit in zazen in
order to get satori.[1]

---

[1]   *Zazen*, simply put, is the primary practice in the Zen schools of Buddhism.
        Literally it could be translated as "sitting-concentration."
            Satori is often translated as "awakening" or "enlightenment." Here,

Every single being simply realizes the self, through the self, for the self.

❦

Religion means living your own life, completely fresh and new, without being deceived by anyone.

❦

Hey! What are you looking at? Don't you see that it's about you?

❦

The asshole doesn't need to be ashamed of being the asshole. The feet don't have any reason to go on strike just because they're only feet. The head isn't the most important of all, and the navel doesn't need to imagine he's the father of all things.

It's strange though that people look at the prime minister as an especially important person. The nose can't replace the eyes, and the mouth can't replace the ears.

Everything has its own identity, which is unsurpassable in the whole universe.

---

and in general when Sawaki Rōshi uses the term, he is critical of a tendency to make it into the goal of zazen practice.

All living things live out their own, unsurpassable identity. Each person can only live out their own life. How can it be that everyone has lost sight of that?

Our society lacks good examples. People who follow so-called "common sense" and "group thinking" and "factionalism" are all only bad examples.

During the Tokugawa Era, the Confucians said, "Shakyamuni was so full of himself! He talked about his identity as unsurpassable in the entire cosmos."

That was their misunderstanding. Not only Shakyamuni has an identity which is unsurpassable in the entire cosmos. Every single one of us has an unsurpassable identity. We moan about it, while all along we're carrying it around with us.

To practice the way of Buddha means to manifest within yourself your own identity, which is unsurpassable in the entire universe.

Stop crying! You whine about how boring you are and how everyone else is so much better than you. Then when things go just a little bit better, you're completely carried away.

These days whenever kids cause trouble, people say their environment is to blame. But what's a good environment? What's a bad one? Is it bad to be born rich? Is it better to be born poor?

Truly bad conditions mean that you have been born a human being without your own self.

You've got to avoid talking about your parents, family tree and background as if they make you something special. Don't show off with your money, your position or your clothing either.

You've got to live your own life, naked and sincere. Religion means living your own life, naked and sincere.

Everyone in the world tries to make themselves important with their relationships and possessions. It's like trying to use the plate to give flavor to a flavorless dish.

This is how the human world has lost sight of itself.

In religion, there's no collective responsibility. It all depends on you.

An ordinary person can lose interest in anything if nobody's watching him do it. If someone's watching, he'll even jump into a fire.[2]

The world shouldn't put on such a show about winning or losing.

I am what I am. No comparison is possible.

---

[2] "Ordinary person" (*bonpu*) is a term that Sawaki Rōshi uses often, not in any sort of elitist way, but as a technical term meaning, roughly, "the opposite of a Buddha."

It already begins in school: giving exams, passing out grades, grouping and scoring people according to their work—how foolish!

What does important and unimportant mean? Is it important to have a good memory? Is someone who has a bad memory a bad person? Aren't there lots of idiots with good memories?

There are some who end up at the bottom of their class and then live out their whole lives feeling like victims. They say their lives have been "screwed up." And it's precisely this attitude that screws up their lives.

Don't be happy about the grades others give you. Take responsibility for yourself. You're happy or you're upset when others praise or criticize you, but you don't even understand yourself.

I've never praised anyone. Everybody already sees their own strengths—and even as better than they really are.

Some children have caught a mouse and now it's writhing in the trap. They're having fun watching how it scrapes its nose till it bleeds and how it rips up its tail. Then in the end, they'll throw it to the cat for food.

If I was sitting in the mouse's place, I'd say to myself, "You damn humans won't have any fun with me!" And I'd simply sit zazen.

The way of Buddha means not looking around. It means being completely one with the present activity.

We don't eat in order to shit. We don't shit in order to make manure. But these days everyone seems to believe that we go to school to prepare for university, and we go to university to get a profession.

There's actually no reason at all to look around. Yet it seems like we've been gazing right and left for ages.

Adults have developed some strange tendencies. They can even make a big deal over a single word. On the other hand, just try sometime to embarrass a baby. You won't be able to do it.

Only adults are so self-conscious that they can fall under a sort of spell, getting embarrassed or angry.

It would be better if we just walked straight ahead.

⁂

Everybody talks about "reality" but there's nothing to it. They're actually just being misled by what they call "reality."

⁂

Some people, their whole life long, never find their own way in life.

⁂

Wherever you look, there's nothing but you. There's nothing anywhere that isn't you.

⁂

Samadhi means being yourself and only yourself. That's "the mind that is naturally pure and clear."

Only in zazen can you be yourself and only yourself. Outside of zazen, you constantly try to be better than the others or to have more fun than the others.

Each one of us is born together with the world and dies together with the world, for everyone carries within himself his own, entirely personal world.

2

To you who think there's something to being "in"

You're always hanging onto others. If somebody's eating French fries, you want French fries too. If somebody's sucking on a candy, you want a candy too. If somebody's blowing on a penny whistle, you scream, "Mommy, buy me a penny whistle too!"

And that doesn't just go for children.

When spring comes, you let spring turn your head. When autumn comes, you let autumn turn your head. Everyone is just waiting for something to turn their head. Some even make a living turning heads—they produce advertising.

People love emotional confusion. Just look at the film posters in front of the cinema: nothing but emotional confusion on their faces. Buddha-dharma means not putting yourself at the mercy of emotional confusion.

In the world, on the other hand, a big fuss is made over nothing.

It goes with being an ordinary person: they can only see with the eyes of collective stupidity.

❦

Being surrounded by heroes and scraping up the courage to play hero yourself—there's nothing heroic about that.

A thief says to his son, "If you don't stop right away with your damned honesty, you'll never be a respectable thief like me. You are a disgrace to the profession!"

❦

In the society of the dishonest, an honest person is held for a fool.

❦

Where groups form, perception is dulled and people stop understanding what's good and what's bad. It isn't that we monks want to withdraw from the world or run away from reality. We simply don't want to go along with this narcosis of our perception.

Since ancient times it has been recommended that you seek your own calling in forests and mountains. Forests and mountains here mean the transparent world.

❦

Don't let yourself be excited by the excitement around you. Don't let your surroundings turn your head.

This is what it means to be wise. Don't let yourself be taken in by any philosophy or any group. Don't bother with anything as dimwitted as people.

⁂

Man makes a clever face and talks about being lord on Earth. At the same time, he doesn't even know where to begin with his own body: he watches sports on television and defends himself by saying that everyone else does it too.[3]

⁂

We live in group stupidity and confuse this insanity with true experience. It is essential that you become transparent to yourself and wake up from this madness.

One at a time, people are still bearable, but when they form cliques, they start to get stupid. They fall into group stupidity. They're so determined to become stupid as a group that they found clubs and pay membership dues. Zazen means taking leave of group stupidity.

⁂

---

[3]   Often, in order to maintain a natural and informal conversational tone, we have often chosen in this translation to use male-gendered language.

You do everything that people praise you for. You run after those who are praised. You are never yourself.

❧

Everyone's talking about common sense, but what do they mean? Don't they simply mean thinking like the others? Thinking what group stupidity dictates?

❧

If you're impressed by name and position, it means you're impressed by the same things that impress everyone else.

❧

An election is a curious thing. Just look at the faces of the people who are voting. It's obvious they don't understand a thing about politics, and they don't know anything about the politicians they're voting for either. Still they're all off to the polls. How odd…

❧

"A monk in layman's clothes" refers to a layman who has left group stupidity behind.

❧

Buddhism is a religion that reduces the congestion of blood in the head. Ordinary people are always getting excited, and their blood is always rushing to their heads.

Whether they stuff themselves or have an empty stomach, whether they see a woman or a man, they're always getting excited and their blood is always rushing all around.

Buddhism reduces this congestion. Buddhism means your blood circulates in a natural way.

3

To you who are totally exhausted from fighting with your spouse

When you're fighting with your husband or wife, you don't realize that the argument is about an illusion. But in zazen, you recognize illusion as illusion.

This is why it is important to look at life with the eyes of zazen.

Whatever you were thinking just now, it's gone already.

The question isn't who's right. You're simply seeing things from different points of view.

Stop trying to be something special and just be what you are. Hold fire. Just sit!

It all begins when we say, "I." Everything that follows is illusion.

Everyone imagines that their ego is something unchangeable, some immovable center point which everything revolves around. There once was a man who said, "Look, everyone is dying except me!"

He's been dead for a long time now.

Blindness means that we don't understand the way things are. If we don't understand things, the best thing would be to stay calm. But no, instead of this we stomp around like a bull in a china shop. That's what makes everything complicated.

Life is one big contradiction. You say, "Did you see what he's done?" When all the while you would have loved to have done it yourself!

Life isn't so easy. Sometimes there's war and the sky is on fire, sometimes you take an afternoon nap by the stove. Sometimes you work the whole night through, sometimes you get drunk with friends.

In the buddha-dharma it is a question of how you can give direction to this life according to the Buddha's teaching.

You're in love with each other? But not for your whole life.

There was a couple who loved each other so much that they attempted suicide together in order to be united in death. One of the two survived and shortly afterwards fell in love all over again.

Humans are truly pitiful.

Beauty is no guarantee for a happy life. There is a woman who is so adored by men that she's already had three children who don't know who their fathers are.

Everybody talks about marrying for love, but isn't it really just marrying for sex? In the end isn't it really only about a penis and a vagina? Why doesn't anybody simply say that he's fallen in love with a vagina?

Take a look sometime at the face of a dog who's just had sex. He just stares into space with strangely empty eyes. It's exactly the same with people. In the beginning they work themselves up into a frenzy, and in the end there's nothing at all.

A man who understands nothing marries a woman who understands nothing, and everyone says, "Congratulations!"

Now that's something I cannot understand.

A man who understands nothing, and everyone says, "Congratulations!"

Family is the place where parents and children, husband and wife simultaneously all get on each other's nerves.

When a child is out of line, the parents curse, "You don't understand anything!" But what are the parents like? Isn't it also true that they don't understand anything either?

Everyone is lost in ignorance.

Everyone is talking about education, but what are we being educated to be? Ordinary citizens, that's all.

The bull is proud of his nose ring. Then with the pack saddle of desire strapped to his back, he lets himself be led around by the nose and moos too. What's strange is that people are happy to put up with the same thing.

People who can't stay still in the face of pleasure, anger, sorrow and satisfaction are like mutts who can't keep from yapping.

When the waves of pleasure, anger, sorrow and satisfaction have quieted down, there's nothing really left to do.

Even funnier than watching the monkeys at the zoo is observing these humans on the loose.

4

To you who have just begun brooding over life

What a shame to have been born a human being and to spend your whole life worrying.

You should reach the point where you can be happy to have been born a human.

⬥

Birth, old age, sickness and death: we can't fool around with these ultimate facts.

⬥

Reality: getting a handle on this must be our goal. Don't get stuck in categories.

⬥

It's strange that not a single person seriously considers his own life.

For ages, we've been carrying around something uncooked. Then we comfort ourselves with the fact that it's the same for the others too. That's what I call group stupidity: thinking that we just have to be like the others.

Satori means creating your own life. It means waking up from group stupidity.

In a part of Manchuria, the carts are pulled by huge dogs.

The driver hangs a piece of meat in front of a dog's nose, and the dog runs like crazy to try to get at it. But of course he can't. He's only thrown his meat after the cart has finally reached its destination. Then in a single gulp, he swallows it down.

It's exactly the same with people and their pay checks. Until the end of the month they run after the salary hanging in front of their noses. Once the salary is paid, they gulp it down, and they're already off: running after the next payday.

Nobody can see further than the end of their nose. Everyone believes that their life somehow has meaning, but they're really no different from swallows: the males gather food, the females sit on the eggs.

Most people aren't following any clear approach to life. They haven't got any approach to life besides stopgap methods, like rubbing lotion on a cramped shoulder.

The question is why are you straining your forehead so much?

※

If you aren't careful, you'll spend your whole life doing nothing besides waiting for your ordinary-person hopes to someday be fulfilled.

※

In the world, people are always saying, "I want to do this, I want to do that." But then when they actually do it, there isn't anything to it at all.

※

You read the advice column in the newspaper, just be careful that you don't end up there with your little problem too!

※

No matter how you look at it, everything in the world revolves around food and sex.

※

Imagine some chicks have found an earthworm and are fighting over it. That's exactly how human society looks.

❧

People in the world only understand what's "useful." And where has that brought us? Nowhere!

❧

It's said that some people are trapped by their money. What is it they do with their money anyway?

❧

The satisfaction everyone in the world looks for is followed by dissatisfaction.
The happiness that the world talks about gives way to unhappiness.

❧

Illusion means not having any direction in life.

Since those lacking direction gather in groups, it's natural that there are gangs who beat each other up. It also isn't any wonder when wars break out for no reason at all.

❧

Humans are beings who make an intelligent face while groping around in the dark.

When you get used to this strange world of impermanence, it seems completely normal to you. Although in fact it's obvious that survival in this impermanent world is more difficult than zazen, it seems to you to be the other way around: as if zazen were harder than life!

We've gotten used to this life. That's the only reason we find it normal.

Even a beggar laughs, even a jackpot winner sooner or later cries again. Money isn't what it's all about.

Everything useful is illusory. No matter how special they seem, useful things are illusory.

Things which are good for nothing, however, aren't so artificial. Nothing can be gained from them.

Everything is relative. Even the most important thing in the world is only relative. What is beyond all this is the absolute.

It's no small matter to be born into this world as a human being.

So what a shame it would be if you went crazy and ended up in an asylum, or if you constantly complained about having no money, or if you lost your mind because you'd just fallen in love, and then were completely overcome with grief because she left you, and so on and so forth.

Now that you've been born as a human being, you should lead a life which is truly worth living.

Buddhism teaches us that it's a joy to be born into this world as a human being.

Samadhi means seriously asking yourself the question, "How must this life be lived?"

Everyone believes that satisfaction doesn't mean anything more than laying on the couch or dozing in a hot spring.

No, satisfaction means being suffused with joy, stability and happiness. Only when you've fully arrived in the present instant will you experience true joy, stability and happiness.

✥

For ordinary people there is only love or hate, profit or loss, good or bad, victory or loss.

In the end, we have to realize that none of that is good for anything, and in the end we come to the practice of zazen— simply practicing what isn't good for anything.

✥

"Ordinary person" is the expression for someone who gropes around in the dark, led astray by confusion. What is this confusion really? In the end it doesn't have any substance. That's why being led astray by confusion is like playing tug-of-war with the clouds.

There's nothing final about winning or losing. So, it's stupid to cry with joy when you win and cry in grief when you lose. The substancelessness, beyond winning and losing, is the true form of all phenomena.

A buddha is someone who untangles what's confused.

A person who understands things is a person who doesn't let himself be misled by his personal fabrications and karma.

People who don't understand things are constantly looking for distraction: sometimes they fall in love, sometimes they get drunk, sometimes they dedicate themselves to reading, sometimes they do their sports. But they do all of this only halfheartedly, in order to somehow deceive themselves.

Spending our daily lives fooling ourselves in this halfhearted way is what's called "life in the floating world." That means that our wobbly legs are carrying us off-track.

All the nations of the world are stupefied with boredom, that's why they say, "Right, left, march in step!" And next thing you know, the children are fighting over their toys again.

People wheeze from exhaustion their whole life long, without even knowing what they're wearing themselves out for. It only seems to them as if they had a goal. In truth, there's absolutely nothing there. Only our grave awaits us.

We can only be at peace when we understand things as they are. When we understand things, we see the universe with a single glance, and the seam between ourselves and the universe vanishes.

We were simply born and we will simply die—and you ask about the meaning of life. You ask what zazen is good for. Whereby you'd have no right to complain if you had died already last year.

Isn't it clear from the start that life is good for nothing? It is simply coming and going, that's all. Your problem is that there's something in you that just can't accept that.

Scientists observe insects in a terrarium eating their food or each other, mating or chirping away. In the same way, we are—in everything we do—under the eye of reality.

5

To you whose life is about money, money and more money

The measure of a man: you give him a little money and immediately he starts to move.

⟜

A man is a simpleton. All he wants is money, health, a career and pretty girls.

⟜

Do you really think it's something special to treat yourself to luxury? I can't understand why the whole world envies the rich.

⟜

I always make fun of the rich who act so important with their money. That's why they don't give any of it to me.

⟜

In the past, much ado was made about auspicious directions. But today we have satellites orbiting around the Earth, and we know that the Earth revolves around the sun. There the directions on the Earth don't play a role anymore.

But what goes for directions is suddenly different when it comes to rich and poor. There we still cling to the belief that it's better to be rich than poor. Whereby in reality, we can't possibly know which is better. The rich also have their worries.

In any case, you can also live without money. No one has come into this world carrying a piggy bank.

⁂

Human happiness and unhappiness don't only depend on money. If the balance in your savings account were a measure of your happiness, it would be a simple matter. Yet it really isn't so.

⁂

Without money, you've got difficulties. Still, you should know that there are more important things than money.

You constantly think about sex. Still, you should know that there are more important things than sex.

⁂

Don't be so helpless that you start saying you need money to live. In this world you can lead a fine life without savings.

⁂

"Work, work! When you work, you get money. When you have money, you can take it easy and still have something to eat."

Compared with such simplistic thinking, Marxism is truly sophisticated.

The humans of the world are so childish—and not only because they hang around in pinball arcades. For much higher stakes, they play at victory or loss, butchering and being butchered.

It's clear what you like: having sex, wining and dining, and making yourself a career without having to make an effort. Running after what you like and running away from what you don't like is what is meant by "wandering around in the impermanent world." Even a rat begins to run if you give him an electric shock.

There are some who believe that they really know how to enjoy life, whereby their only pleasure in life is eating well.

We were taught in school to earn a lot of money. What we unfortunately weren't taught is that money makes you dumb.

❧

The rich are rich because money is important to them. That's why they don't give any of it away.

❧

Some think they're important because they have money. Others think they're important because they have "satori." But no matter much how much you puff up your personal sack of flesh, you won't end up becoming anything besides a monster.

That which can't be made into an individual possession fills the entire universe. Where personal thoughts come to an end is where the buddha-dharma begins.

❧

In the world, it's always about winning or losing, plus or minus. Yet in zazen, it's about nothing. It's good for nothing. That's why it is the greatest and most all-inclusive thing there is.

Dōgen says:

The flowers that bejewel the sky of my heart,
I offer them to the buddhas of the three worlds.

– 6 –

To you who think the prime minister is a really special person

So you think someone is "good"? The question is simply, good for what?

In every age, people have been misused and misled by politicians.

We act as if it is our eccentricities that make up our true nature.

Isn't it clear that you're a thief as soon as you steal someone's property? Yet today everyone seems to believe that you aren't guilty as long as you haven't been caught by the police, interrogated by the inspector, convicted by the judge and finally locked up in a cell.

The same goes for corrupt politicians: as long as they can hide all evidence to the contrary, they consider themselves to be competent and successful. That shows how far group stupidity has taken us.

Even when the Chinese Emperor was surrounded by shrewd advisors, he always had enough "wisdom" to mislead them. This type of wisdom has nothing to do with the wisdom of the buddha-dharma.

You don't have to be a Goemon Ishikawa to be a thief.[4] Even somebody who's stolen something only once, on a whim, is still a complete thief.

In the same way, Shakyamuni isn't the only buddha. Everyone who imitates Buddha's zazen is a complete buddha.

We all develop peculiar habits. The powerful, and the teachers and intellectuals who serve them, do their best to train us in these peculiarities. In this way we are tied and twisted in the most complicated ways. Religion means untying these knots.

In the end, there is only emptiness.

---

[4] Goemon Ishikawa (1568-1594) was a famous Japanese thief who, together with his gang and family, was put to death by being cooked alive in boiling water. His life provided material for many historical dramas in Japan.

Everyone is trying to make themselves out to be important according to their worldly criteria.

Everyone is trying to make themselves out to be important according to their worldly criteria.

What one system built, the other will destroy. What one political power accomplished will be repealed by the next.

A person who seeks his true calling won't want to pursue a career. A person who wants to become president doesn't know where he's going in life.

Their election is so important to them that presidents and congressmen campaign to rally votes. Idiots! Even if they asked me to become president, I'd turn it down. How dumb do you think I am anyway?

One guy loses the presidential election, so he cries. Next time around he wins the election, and then he smiles into the camera. What makes politicians different from little children anyway? It's exactly the same way with a crying child: you offer him some candy and already a smile breaks out on his teary face.

A little more maturity would be nice.

Anyone who relies on his resume is a failure.

Most people don't live from their own strength. They let themselves be fed by the system.

"He's a great guy: he can drink two bottles of wine just like that!" What's called "good" is usually nothing special. Each clique has their own standard which they use to explain something as "good" or "not so good."

People are impressed by strange things. You only need to be a little different and the whole world is impressed.

Some are strong, like lions. Others are long, like snakes. Others can see even at night, like weasels. Some have their young stolen one after the other, until the day when someone breaks their neck, like chickens. Some are taken advantage of their whole lives long, and in the end they are slaughtered and eaten, even the bones and the skin are put to use, like cows. Others always have a place on a woman's lap, where they're happy, like tomcats. All of that is karma. It is neither good nor bad.

In the end, a person whose karma is too good falls headfirst into hell.

⁂

What could be more boring than showing off your skills? Skills are only relative: they're not really worth anything. What lies beyond your talents, that's what matters.

⁂

When you look at heroes, East and West, past and present, you can clearly see that the strong as well as the weak didn't do anything besides exhaust themselves and die in the end. They all gave everything they had, wearing themselves out for an illusion and accumulating bad karma.

⁂

All beings are blind to the dharma. And that doesn't just go for delinquents and gangsters. Children who are born blind to the dharma are raised by blind parents, educated by blind teachers and misled by politicians who are blind to the dharma. How could anyone around here not be blind to the dharma?

<hr />

Once there was a great madman in the Sugamo hospital who called himself "Ashiwara Shōgun." He hung a cardboard medal around his neck and bestowed dignified words to those he met to take with them on their way. Now that the war is over, we can see clearly that what the military did wasn't at all different.

<hr />

After winning the Russo-Japanese war, we thought we'd won colonies. But what really came of it? After losing the Second World War, we realized that we had only earned the hatred of the Russians.

<hr />

Everyone is talking about loyalty to the fatherland. The question is simply where this loyalty will take us. I too was completely convinced when I went to war against the Russians, but after our defeat, I realized that we had done something that we shouldn't have. In any case, it's better not to make war in the first place.

The life and death of many depends on whether a single Stalin is born or not. Whether a single person is born or not makes a huge difference. That's why it is so significant that the one person, Shakyamuni, was born.

People are good as they originally are, but unfortunately they drift off in the wrong direction. That's because they follow bad examples.

The Buddhist school, *Sōkagakkai,* promises you happiness, but where is this happiness supposed to come from? From earning money, they say! But what does money have to do with happiness anyway? Didn't Shakyamuni renounce his palace and throne and beg for his meals?[5]

Losing your balance because of happiness and unhappiness is what's called "illusion."

---

[5]   Traditionally, since the Buddha's time, monks have received donations of food or money given by lay people.

Everybody's karma is different. What's important is the fact that everyone is pulled forward by Buddha in the same way.

Dropping off body and mind means to stop wearing yourself out, and instead to trust in Buddha, to let yourself be pulled by Buddha.

7

To you who would like to leave your rivals in the dust

We often wonder who here is really better? But aren't we all made out of the same lump of clay?

Everyone should sit firmly anchored in the place where there is no better and worse.

Your whole life long you're completely out of your mind because you think it's obvious that there is a "you" and "the others." You put on an act to stand out in a crowd, but in reality there's neither "you" nor "the others."

When you die, you'll understand.

Buddha-dharma means seamlessness. What seam runs between you and me? Sooner or later we all end up acting as if a seam separates friend and foe.

Poor and rich, important and unimportant—none of that exists. It's only glitter on the waves.

There's nothing in the world we need to rack our brains over once it's clear that our deluded and discriminating thoughts are absolutely useless.

When the department head was sick, a subordinate jumped past him on the career ladder. He had been recovering, but with this news his fever broke out again. You really don't need to get a fever over something like that.

You say, "I'll show you!" Yet you don't even know how long you'll live. Don't you have anything else to do?

In the West they say, "Man is the wolf of man." The first step in religion must be that the wolves stop biting each other.

What we've learned since our childhood days is nothing more than how to pretend we're important. The world calls this education.

And what do we try to do later in life? We fight like demons, have sex like animals and feed like the hungry ghosts. That's it.

People make a sleepy face if there isn't a fight or competition taking place. They're always wanting to gallop to the finish line. But is this a horse race? Or they swim like otters, wanting to be a nose ahead. In the end, they'll fight each other, like little kittens over a ball of wool.

In the buddha-dharma it isn't about winning or losing, love or hate.

Some want to show off with their "satori." Yet it's clear that something which you can use to show off has nothing to do with real satori.

8

To you who are sobbing because somebody's put one over on you

At some point you've got to slap yourself in the face and seriously ask yourself: is your personal gain or loss really worth being overwhelmed by joy and suffering?

Sooner or later everyone starts thinking of nothing besides themselves.

You say, "That was good!" But what was good? It was only good for you personally, that's all.

Why is it that we humans are so exhausted?
It is the constant effort to gain a little advantage that exhausts us.

Illusion means being unstable. Illusion means being controlled by the situation.

A person with big desires is easily fooled. Even the greatest conman can't profit from a person with no desires.

⁂

Buddhism means no self, nothing to gain. You must be one with the universe and all living beings.

⁂

Non-self means not turning your back on people.

⁂

All beings are mistaken. We see as happiness that which leads to unhappiness, and weep over an unhappiness which isn't unhappiness at all.

We all know the child whose tears suddenly turn into laughter when you give him a cookie. What we living beings call happiness isn't much more than that.

⁂

We often say, "I saw it with my own eyes, heard it with my own ears!" We act as if this was the firmest foundation there is, but these eyes and ears are not to be trusted at all. Everyone is deceived by their eyes, ears, nose, tongue, body and mind.

There are some who cheat on the preparatory exam, so they have to cheat on the real exam as well, otherwise they won't pass. They go so far with their stupidity that I almost owe them my respect. But actually, if you think about it, you find the same sort of stupidity everywhere in this world.

It's difficult to drink in moderation. That's because it's the wine itself that drinks the wine. It's exactly the same with the illusions in the world.

Take a hundred thousand possibilities, line them up and compare them: they all lead down a dead end. This way leads down a dead end, that way leads down a dead end. Whatever direction you go in, you are stuck.

Now simply throw out everything that would lead down a dead end. What's left?

A man of great leisure, beyond learning and doing. (Shōdōka)

– 9 –

To you who would like to slap your boss with a
letter of resignation

As a human being, you can walk freely in any direction you choose.

⁂

As a human being, whatever you do, you should do it in a way that can't be done a second time. What can be repeated is best left to the robots.

⁂

Life doesn't run on tracks.

⁂

Birds don't sing in a major or minor key. Bodhidharma's teaching doesn't fit on lined paper.

The buddha-dharma is wide and unlimited. When you try to hold it still, you've missed it. It isn't dried cod, but a live fish—and living fish have no fixed form.

⁂

In the soldier's handbook it says that in war you must be prepared for a thousand different possibilities. That doesn't just go for war. There's no rule book for life either.

When you try to live your life according to a manual, you're sure to fail.

❧

The wild geese leave no traces,
yet no matter where they fly, they never lose their way.

There are no footprints on the way of the bird. It's not the same as a steam engine that runs on tracks or an ox's well-worn path.

❧

Don't we live life from moment to moment? How could we possibly take life, analyze it, systematize it and file it away?

❧

The sad thing about people is that they can't stray even a single step away from their habits.

❧

We constantly let ourselves be distracted by details, and in this way we lose sight of the whole.

We buy strange things that we don't want at all in the hope that we just might win something with the lottery ticket the cashier gives us for free.

Actually, "studying" used to mean gaining insight into life, but now it's turned into just getting qualifications for a job.

However much you accomplish in this life, in the end you won't have anything to show for it. You will die naked.

In the world, isn't what we call good or bad, true or false, more or less the same thing?

You've got to stand on solid feet, no matter what direction the wind might blow.

Isn't it evident that the greatest happiness consists in doing what you have to do?

❦

Not wasting your time in life means sitting stably in the right place at the right time—not missing the precise moment.

❦

You can't depend on anything. The value of things changes. This insight is what motivated Shakyamuni to renounce his King's title, to leave his wife and son and become a monk.

– 10 –

To you who wants to begin with zazen

In the world you'll find all kinds of rewards, but is there any reward that could make you happier than settling your bottom onto your sitting cushion and having the privilege to practice zazen?

If you prefer to believe in this or that other sect, go and follow them. Only those who really want to practice zazen should do so.

What is zazen good for? Zazen is good for absolutely nothing!

Dōgen Zenji had something against large numbers of followers. He said they're like "flies and worms." They're nothing compared to a single dragon or a single elephant. That's why Zen monks are also called dragons and elephants.

Once there were 500 monkeys in the service of 500 Buddhist *arhats*.[6] One day the monkeys decided to mimic everything the arhats did, so they did zazen copying them with their eyes, noses, mouths and whole bodies. They say that in this way a thousand arhats practiced zazen and realized awakening. This is why it's my wish to preserve—even if it's only through imitation—the seed of zazen.

When you practice zazen, completely renew yourself.

When you practice Zen, it has to be here and now, it has to be about yourself. Don't let Zen become a rumor that has nothing to do with you.

Right next to Komazawa University's zazen hall is the baseball field. When you hear the cheerleaders practicing before their games, you can truly understand how much we neglect the self.

---

[6] An *arhat* is traditionally understood as a person who has gained insight into the true nature of existence and has achieved nirvana. Here Sawaki makes the point that nirvana is not achieved through insight, but rather expresses itself in the daily conduct of a practitioner. (Based in part: https://en.wikipedia .org/wiki/Arhat)

Zazen is the buddha that we form out of our raw flesh.

Just sitting (*shikantaza*)[7] is the greatest thing that we can do with the raw flesh of an ordinary person.

The Chinese character for "pelvis/hips" (*koshi*) is composed of the character for "flesh" on the left side and "essential" on the right side. In zazen, from the beginning, it is essential that the pelvis is firmly anchored on the cushion.

In zazen, the hips are rooted in the Earth, the top of the head pierces the sky.

---

[7]   *Shikantaza* is the key practice in the teaching of Dōgen Zenji and Sawaki Rōshi. Essentially it is simply sitting single-mindedly in the posture of zazen. Though sometimes called meditation, it can be distinguished from other mediation practices in that there is no mental object (mantra, visualization, kōan etc.) that is meditated upon, and in that there is no goal to the practice.

When you practice zazen in a place where you can hear sounds that arouse pleasure, anger, sorrow or contentment, the waves they create in your mind keep zazen from soaking into your flesh and bones.

If you're looking for stimulation in zazen, you've been hanging out with the wrong crowd. In zazen, you have to eliminate all stimulation and not practice anything special at all.

The body that takes a nap can also practice zazen.

The body that practices zazen can also take a nap.

To practice zazen together for an entire day is an extraordinary opportunity.

To spend the whole day with prostitutes is extraordinary stupidity.

If you eat in the evening in order to break into a house afterwards, you are eating a "robbery-meal." If you eat in order to go to the prostitutes, you are eating a "prostitute-meal." If you eat to practice zazen, then it is a meal of the Buddha way.

The question is why do you eat?

When we change the mattresses at Antaiji, it's not the same thing as when the madam of a brothel changes her mattresses. For the madam, it's about luring customers and making money. For us, it's so the people who come to practice zazen don't catch colds.

Whoever comes to practice zazen is a buddha. He sleeps on a buddha's mattress.

Eat in order to do zazen, sleep in order to do zazen. This means that eating and sleeping are also part of zazen.

When you think about earning your living during zazen, you start saying things like, "Working is also Zen, sitting is also Zen." And you stop sitting zazen.

When you say, on the other hand, that only zazen is important, then you start thinking that only zazen is zazen, and that everything else has nothing to do with zazen.

In our practice, there's nothing sacred besides zazen. It's zazen that saves us ordinary beings by taking our raw flesh and molding it into zazen.

Only buddha together with buddha can discuss the buddha-dharma, buddha and an ordinary person cannot. That's why it says in the *Lotus Sutra*, "Only a buddha together with a buddha can penetrate it."

In the same way, the mind shared by buddha and buddha is only realized by sitting upright, facing the wall.

Our zazen is like waking up from hibernation to a completely new world.

Zazen means returning once again to the womb. That's why zazen isn't "work."

⁂

Everyone is so busy with their calculations that they even forget what they were calculating in the first place. Zazen means stopping with all of this calculating.

⁂

Zazen means graduating from all human hallucinations.

⁂

Zazen means practicing that which cannot be explained.

⁂

Zazen means putting into practice that which cannot be thought.

⁂

Your zazen alone penetrates heaven and earth. It certifies this place of great liberation.

⁂

Zazen is the dharma-switch that turns on the whole universe.

Samadhi means practicing that which fills the entire universe, throwing yourself into it completely, in every single instant, in every single activity.

"Simply doing" means doing it now, on the spot. It means not wasting the little time you have in life.

"Myself and all living beings on Earth realize the way together." (Shakyamuni Buddha)

In the buddha-dharma this isn't enforced with political power. "I, myself" put it into practice.

When you sit, you've got to be one with Truman, Stalin and Mao. One person sits for everyone, everyone sits as one.

The phenomenal world isn't something that some god made. It arises through interdependent causation.

Buddha is an immeasurable cause resulting in an immeasurable effect. Thinking from the basis of non-thinking—this is how buddha is actualized.

It's often said that Zen means non-mind. Non-mind refers to that which is immeasurable, and this "immeasurable" is more than just the opposite of measurable.

Apart from zazen, all of your "good deeds" come out of your ego-consciousness, because you're always thinking, "I do good."

Only when you stop thinking "I do zazen" are you doing true zazen.

Sit in zazen with the intention to starve.

That means that you shouldn't count on "always having something to eat as long as the wheel of the dharma turns." On the contrary, as long as you keep the wheel of the dharma turning, it doesn't matter at all whether you have something to eat or not.

❧

What caters to worldly feelings has nothing to do with zazen.

The buddha-dharma doesn't care a whit about what we humans would prefer.

❧

"What's this all about? All these people sitting around staring at the wall? What could be more absurd?"

That's how zazen appears to people stuck in the impermanent world.

❧

"What is zazen good for?"

This question itself is really good for nothing. What has the invention of the television been good for? And what have you been good for? Isn't everything actually good for nothing?

❧

When somebody asks me what zazen is good for, I say that zazen isn't good for anything at all. Then some say that in that case they'd rather stop doing zazen.

But what's running around satisfying your desires good for? What is gambling good for? And dancing? What is it good for to get worked up over winning or losing in baseball? It's all good for absolutely nothing! That's why nothing is as sensible as sitting silently in zazen.

In the world, "good for nothing" just means that you can't make money out of it.

Often people ask me how many years they have to practice zazen before it shows results.

Zazen has no results. You won't get anything at all out of zazen.

Recently we've been experiencing here a Zen boom. In every magazine there's something written about Zen, but when you read it, you only find a bunch of strange ideas. Some write about what they picked up somewhere second-hand. Some give an account of a one-week seminar with guaranteed "*kenshō*."[8]

---

[8]   *Kenshō* is a dramatic awakening experience.

The problem is that people who have never heard anything about Zen can be misled by such nonsense.

✿

If you don't have a clear, Buddhist approach to life, it would be better if you kept away from zazen practice.

✿

Nenbutsu practiced with a peaceful mind is true *nenbutsu*.[9] Zazen practiced with a peaceful mind is genuine zazen.

Nenbutsu practiced in order to get peace of mind isn't true *nenbutsu*. Zazen practiced in order to get peace of mind isn't true zazen.

When eating as well, Buddha's practice is perfecting the meal through a perfected manner of eating.

---

[9] Simply put, *nenbutsu* is the practice of reciting the name of a buddha, often in the belief that this will lead to going to the Pure Land after death.

11

To you who wants to strengthen your hara *with zazen*

"Through zazen you strengthen your *hara*."[10]

Knowing that this hara isn't worth a damn is real hara and real zazen.

Some try to become thick-skinned through zazen.

If it's even the slightest bit personalized, it isn't pure, unadulterated zazen.

We've got to practice genuine, pure zazen, without mixing it with gymnastics or satori or anything. When we bring in our personal ideas—even only a little bit—it's no longer the buddha-dharma.

In a word, Buddhism is non-self. Non-self means that "I" am not a separate subject. When "I" am not a separate subject, then I fill the entire universe.

---

[10]   The *hara* is an area in the lower abdomen, considered is East Asia to be a center of energy.

In true dharma there's nothing to gain.
In false dharma there's something to gain.

If you practice zazen when you are overwhelmed by feelings
of pleasure, anger, sorrow and contentment, these feelings
will haunt your zazen like a terrible ghost.

The way of Buddha means that there is nothing to seek,
nothing to find. If there's something to find, no matter how
much we practice, it's got nothing to do with the buddha-
dharma. If there's nothing to find, that's the buddha-dharma.

Whatever it is you're trying to grasp, even if you get it, sooner
or later you'll lose it again.

True wealth is not grasping for anything. It's shining our light
inwards and reflecting upon ourselves. When we take a step
back, we see that there's nothing to grasp, nothing to run
after and nothing to run away from. Reality doesn't arise and
doesn't pass, it's neither pure nor impure, it neither increases
nor decreases.

A monk, Yakuzan, is practicing zazen and his teacher, Master Sekitō, asks him, "What are you doing there?"

"I'm not doing anything at all."

"If you're not doing anything at all, does that mean that you're just passing the time?"

"If I were passing the time, then I'd be doing something, but I'm not even doing that."

"You say you're doing nothing. What is it that you're not doing?"

"Even a thousand wise men couldn't know it."

Nothing is as still and noble as this zazen that even a thousand wise men couldn't know, the zazen which Yakuzan practiced and Master Sekitō praised.

These days there are some masters who you can sit with for a week, and for a nice sum of money you're guaranteed a *kenshō* experience. It's obvious that anything like that has nothing to do with Yakuzan's zazen which even a thousand wise men couldn't know. Sitting and practicing that which even a thousand wise men couldn't know is the meaning of simply sitting, shikantaza.

These days there's a lot of talk about zazen. The question is simply, what are they trying to do with their zazen? Some toil away to cultivate their *hara,* to become stronger personalities, to get satori and so on and so forth. The little monks even call *kōan* training a "guessing game."

All this is nothing more than buddha-dharma from the point of view of ordinary people. But the buddha-dharma isn't a dharma for ordinary people. We've got to observe the buddha-dharma with the eyes of the buddha-dharma. That's why it is so rare that zazen itself truly practices zazen.

Some people want to use zazen to become better people. Zazen for them is nothing more than make-up.

This isn't an educational institution here! What we are trying to do is to become a blank slate. Here there's nothing to gain. Here's a place where you have to let go of all illusion and awakening.

The buddha-dharma isn't about making average people into special people.

Zazen takes place when you stop elbowing the others to get ahead.

***

You go swimming every morning in cold water? So what? A goldfish does that all the time.

You've quit smoking? Yeah, so what? A cat doesn't smoke either.

However proud you are of how well you run after this and run away from that, it's nothing more than wandering around in the world of impermanence.

***

True religion is seeing the world as it is, free of all fabrications.

***

Everything is good as it is. We don't need to fool around with it.

***

However unusual and mystical your experiences may be, they won't last your whole life long. Sooner or later they'll fade away.

⁂

Ordinary people really go for miracles and magic. They love hocus-pocus.

⁂

Ordinary people by nature don't like practice, they only want satori. They want to earn money without working. That's why they form lines at lottery windows.

They don't want the true dharma, but they swarm towards the new sects that promise heaven on earth.

⁂

You get stuck on satori, you get stuck on money, you get stuck on your position and reputation, you get stuck on sex.

Not getting stuck is what's meant by the buddha-dharma.

12

To you who is wondering if your zazen has been good for something

What's zazen good for?

Absolutely nothing! This "good for nothing" has got to sink into your flesh and bones until you're truly practicing what's good for nothing. Until then, your zazen is really good for nothing.

Throwing yourself completely into doing what's good for absolutely nothing—why not give it a try?

So you say you'd like to try doing zazen in order to become a better person. Become a better person by doing zazen? How ridiculous! How could a person ever become something better?

You say you want to become a better person by doing zazen.

Zazen isn't about learning how to be a person. Zazen is to stop being a person.

Some say, "Zen means having an empty mind, right?"
You won't have an empty mind until you're dead.

⬧

They think that with zazen everything gets better.
Foolish! Zazen means forgetting "better" and "worse."

⬧

You are not going to earn tips doing zazen.
The day is as long as a child's day.
The mountain is as quiet as the eternal past.

⬧

Zazen is unsatisfying. Unsatisfying for whom? For the
ordinary person. People are never satisfied.

⬧

In our Sōtō school, zazen isn't so exciting. Ordinary people
are always looking for excitement—sports, gambling on
horse races and things like that. What makes them so
popular? It's the excitement of winning and losing.

⬧

Isn't it self-evident? How could that which is eternal and infinite ever satisfy human desires?

⌇

Unsatisfying: simply practicing zazen.
Unsatisfying: realizing zazen with this body.
Unsatisfying: absorbing zazen into your flesh and blood.

⌇

Being watched by zazen, cursed by zazen, blocked by zazen, dragged around by zazen, every day crying tears of blood— isn't that the happiest form of life you can imagine?

⌇

Somebody asks, "I can understand that during zazen we're buddhas. But does that mean that we are just ordinary people when we are not doing zazen?"

When a thief steals, he's a thief. If for a moment he isn't stealing anything, does that mean that he isn't a thief anymore?

Is eating in order to steal and eating in order to practice zazen the same thing or are they different?

Somebody who steals once isn't trusted anymore. Somebody who practices zazen once practices eternal zazen.

Zazen is really an amazing thing. When you are sitting, it doesn't seem like zazen is anything particularly good. But when you see it from the outside, there's nothing that could be so majestic.

With everything else, it's usually the other way around. Looked at objectively, there's not much to it. You're the only one who thinks what you are doing is so terribly important.

The reason the buddha-dharma fills the whole universe is because it doesn't offer anything you can grab onto.

Making a constant effort isn't difficult if you don't grab onto anything.

Zazen is transparent. It has no flavor. When we give zazen a flavor, it becomes something for ordinary people.

Zazen isn't so fashionable. What's fashionable is what comes natural for an ordinary person, like the fight over winning and losing in sports.

Zazen isn't fashionable because it's flavorless and ungraspable. It doesn't interest childish people.

The immense, transparent sky isn't the same thing as a bonsai tree or little statues for your little altar. It's infinitely vast.

Nonetheless, people prefer trimming around on their bonsai trees or tending to their little statues.

You want flavoring for your consciousness. That's why you're not impressed by the transparent, tasteless buddha-dharma.

You say, "When I do zazen, I get disturbing thoughts!"

Foolish! The fact is that it's only in zazen that you're aware of your disturbing thoughts at all. When you dance around with your disturbing thoughts, you don't notice them at all.

When a mosquito bites you during zazen, you notice it right away. But when you're dancing and a flea bites your balls, you don't notice it at all.

A layman asked: "I've been practicing zazen for a long time, but I still have many disturbing thoughts, and I don't know what to do about it. Only once, during an air raid, when bombs were going off, I did zazen and didn't have a single disturbing thought. I'd never had such a good zazen. Still, afterwards everything was like it was before. Isn't there any way to practice a zazen like that again?"

Sawaki Rōshi answered: "Yes, kōan Zen.[11] Someone gives you a kōan and yells you into a corner. Then there's no room for disturbing thoughts. But still afterwards everything will be like it was before. You've just pushed your disturbing thoughts aside for a moment.

"On the other hand, in Dōgen Zenji's shikantaza, it's about completely manifesting your true form. Your ugliness is exposed, and you see yourself for who you really are. You realize that you're constantly producing disturbing thoughts, just like a crab blows bubbles.

"In fact, it's a merit of zazen to be able to see that you're full of disturbing thoughts. When you're completely preoccupied with something, nothing else comes to mind. With a drink in your hand and your arm around a geisha, you don't feel the flea biting you at all. For that instant all your thoughts are

---

11   Simply put, in kōan Zen, one meditates intently a traditional Zen dialogue (a kōan) in order to have a dramatic awakening experience (kenshō). This is often contrasted with shikantaza, "simply sitting" without object or goal, in which practice and awakening are seen as one.

pushed aside. During zazen, though, you're so aware of this flea that you don't know what to do with yourself. Because in zazen, you aren't numb. You've become transparent and clear."

Isn't it natural that in the course of our lives we'll experience all kinds of psychological phenomena?

We have all kinds of thoughts during zazen, and we wonder if that's correct. The fact that we can ask ourselves this proves that the nature of zazen is pure, and that this pure nature is looking us in the eye. When we dance around drunk in our underwear, we don't question ourselves at all.

Zazen is the unity of Buddha and this ordinary person.

At precisely this moment, you can see yourself with the eyes of Buddha, and it's clear how imperfect you really are—in light of the fact that you are originally a buddha.

It's only the ordinary person in you who is disturbed by disturbing thoughts.

Don't whine. Don't stare into space. Just sit!

13

To you who says that you have attained a better state of mind
through zazen

As long as you say zazen is a good thing, something isn't
quite right. Unstained zazen is absolutely nothing special. It
isn't even necessary to be grateful for it.

Wouldn't it be strange if a baby said to its mother, "Please
have understanding for the fact that I'm always shitting in my
diapers."

Without knowledge, without consciousness, everything is as
it should be.

Don't stain your zazen by saying that you've progressed, feel
better, or have become more confident through zazen.

❧

We only say, "Things are going well!" when they're going our
way.

❧

We should simply leave the water of our original nature as
it is. But instead we are constantly mucking about with our
hands to find out how cold or warm it is. That's why it gets
cloudy.

There are bodhisattvas "without magical abilities." These are bodhisattvas who have even entirely forgotten words like "practice" or "satori," bodhisattvas without wonderful powers, bodhisattvas who are immeasurable, bodhisattvas who are not interested in their name and fame.

Zazen isn't like a thermometer where the temperature slowly rises: "Just a little more … yeah … that's it! Now, I've got satori!" Zazen never becomes anything special, no matter how long you practice.

If it becomes something special, you must have a screw lose somewhere.

There are some who can even delude themselves with their zazen. They reckon that the temperature on their Zen thermometer is already quite high. But this has nothing to do with zazen. "Simply doing" it (*shikan*) is zazen.

The same is also true for *nenbutsu*. You shouldn't practice *nenbutsu* in order to go to paradise some day. You should simply do it. This means simply doing what Buddha does.

We can't save up on zazen.

"I was so very honest when I was still young, that I've decided, now that I'm old, that I can steal things from others from time to time." We can't save up on honesty either.

❦

If we don't watch out, we'll start believing that the buddha-dharma is like climbing up a staircase. But it isn't like this at all.

This very step right now is the one practice which includes all practices, and it is all practices, contained in this one practice.

❦

You say you're finished with practice. From a religious point of view, there's nothing more absurd.

❦

The true satori of the buddha-dharma has got to fill all time, all space, heaven and earth. One or two little satoris that we pick like apples or pears aren't worth a fart.

❦

If you do something good, you can't forget you've done something good. If you've had satori, you get stuck in the awareness of having satori. That's why it's better to keep your hands off good deeds and satori. You've got to be perfectly open and free. Don't rest on your laurels!

Even if I say all of this about the Buddha way, ordinary people will still use the buddha-dharma to try and enhance their value as humans.

When there's an opposition between purity and impurity, that leads to a fight between purity and impurity. You've got to go beyond purity and impurity.

Zazen is good: because zazen is the posture of the person who has experienced great death.[12]

---

[12] "Great death" is an expression for having left behind all attachments.

14

To you who do everything you can to get satori

We don't practice in order to get satori. It's satori that pulls our practice. We practice, being dragged all over by satori.

⁂

You don't seek the way. The way seeks you.

⁂

You study, you do sports, and you're fixated on satori and illusion. Even zazen becomes a marathon for you, with satori as the finish line. Yet because you're trying to grab it, you're missing it completely.

Only when you stop meddling like this does your original, universal nature realize itself.

⁂

You say you're seeking the way, but what does it mean if you're seeking the way just to satisfy yourself?

⁂

Running after satori and running away from illusion is buying and selling shares of one and the same company.

Doing zazen because you want to become buddha or get satori is running after an object.

Zazen is to stop wanting to become buddha or experience satori.

Being beyond-thinking has nothing to do with seeking satisfaction. It means being firmly settled in the here-and-now.

The buddha-dharma cannot be attained by human effort.

Outside of a special clique, saying, "We must attain satori!" is just as strange as saying, "We must behold God!"

The buddha-dharma doesn't mean personal satisfaction. That's why Shakyamuni said, "Myself and everything living on the Earth attain the way together. Mountains, rivers, grasses and trees are all buddha."

The buddha-dharma isn't about trying to get some personal satori.

People want even their satori made to order.

The buddha-dharma means egolessness.

Everyone has their own personal ego. But it's completely backwards to try—especially in zazen—to get a personal satori. Egolessness isn't something personal.

So you want your own personal satori, some sort of peace of mind only for yourself?

Do you really think the buddha-dharma exists just for you?

If you aren't careful, you might start thinking that your individuality is the most important thing in the world. Then you forget that which fills the whole universe.

When I say "satori," you think that I'm talking about some personal satori. So let's get it straight: real satori is what you can't even call "satori."

You want to become a buddha? There's no need to become a buddha!

Now is simply now. You are simply you.

And tell me, since you want to leave the place where you are: where is it exactly you want to go?

Wanting to become a buddha by practicing zazen is like sitting in a train and being in such a hurry to get home that you get up and start running inside the train.

🍃

"Getting satori through practice": that's how the world likes to imagine it. But no matter what sutra you read, you'll never find anything of the sort. No buddha has ever become a buddha through practice. Buddhas have been buddhas from the beginning.

🍃

We don't start practicing now in order to get satori later. Every single one of us has always been a buddha, lacking nothing. It's just that somewhere along the line we've forgotten that. We've lost our way, and now we get all worked up over nothing.

Our practice means nothing besides practicing being the buddha who we have really always been.

꧁

The just sitting (shikantaza) practiced by the buddhas and ancestors does not mean striving to become a buddha.

If you believe that buddha or satori exists outside of zazen, and you think that you can strive towards this, you're mistaking yourself for something special. Buddhist practice means putting buddha into practice.

꧁

When you sit zazen, you attain the way without thinking at all about attaining the way.

꧁

We don't achieve satori through practice. Practice *is* satori. Each and every step is the goal.

꧁

We've got to go all the way with our practice. Who cares if some satori is waiting for us as a reward or not?

❧

Most people have lost their soul. They don't move a muscle unless they're paid or praised, and if you don't hold any satori in front of their noses, they won't practice either.

❧

Master Seigen Gyōshi asked the Sixth Ancestor, "What practice goes beyond ranks and stages?"

The Sixth Ancestor responds, "What have you been doing the whole time?"

Seigen answers, "I'm not even practicing the noble truths."

That means, "I haven't even had satori."

The Sixth Ancestor expressed his deep approval, "When you don't even practice the noble truths, what ranks and stages could there still be?"[13]

The world is full of ranks and stages: rich and poor, important and unimportant. What goes beyond all this is the buddha-dharma.

---

[13] From *The Jingde Record of the Transmission of the Lamp*, a multi-volume work consisting of reputed biographies of the Chan Buddhist and Zen Buddhist patriarchs and other prominent Buddhist monks.

In zazen there is no better and worse, no ranks and stages. Only when you practice zazen to get satori are there ranks and stages.

⬦

A person gets satori: that's something people can talk about. What people don't talk about is zazen.

⬦

Dropping off body and mind means that individual practice and individual satori disappear.

⬦

It seems there are some who try to put the buddha-dharma to work for people. It's just like how everyone these days is interested in self-improvement. They are trying to improve themselves with their practice and get satori.

Yet it's clear that until we give up this human ambition, there can't be any dropping off of body and mind.

⬦

The buddha-dharma is ungraspable. So don't grasp for it. Let go.

What are you grasping for anyway? You think you've got something in your hand, but look: you're holding onto horseshit.

Because you try to make things your own, you're lost in the labyrinth of transmigration.

⬨

To say that illusion or satori exists, that's the way the world gossips—that's something they can grasp.

The buddha-dharma cannot be grasped. It's beyond all that.

⬨

Distinguishing between illusion and satori is human work.

The buddha-dharma doesn't mean destroying illusions to get satori. Zazen means not running after and not running away.

⬨

The buddha-dharma is limitless. If you don't understand this limitlessness, you won't understand the buddha-dharma.

What's more, if you think in terms of understanding or not understanding, you completely miss the point of limitlessness.

That's why there is no illusion outside of satori and no satori outside of illusion.

15

To you who is showing off your satori

Why don't you simply have "I have satori!" tattooed all over your body?

If you're not conscious of your stomach, that's proof your stomach is healthy. If you can't forget your satori, that's proof that you haven't got any.

⁂

When an ordinary person has got satori, he's called a Zen-devil. That's because he thinks he's something special.

⁂

When you know you're doing something bad, then it isn't so serious. But people who chat about their satori don't even realize they're doing something bad. That's why they're such helpless cases.

⁂

Some people are detested by their entire family and still believe that only they are in the right. If you think you're the only one who's right, you're wrong. That goes even more for certain Zen laymen who think their satori makes them so important—even if they're hated at home.

No illusion is as hard to cure as satori.

The monk Gon'yō asks Jōshū, "How is it when not a single thing appears anymore?"

Jōshū answers, "Let it go!"

Gon'yō asks, "For me, not a single thing appears anymore, what should I let go?"

Jōshū answers, "If that's how it is, then get out of here—and take it with you!"

Don't take pride in your practice. It's clear that any satori you take pride in is a lie.

When superficial people do something wrong, they don't notice it until they've been caught by the police. Not to notice that you're living in an illusion goes with being an ordinary person.

You need to see clearly.

Real satori means manifesting your sobriety. It means coming to your senses. The more you look, the more clearly you see your faults as well.

🍂

Sudden great satori means that all the old conceptions drop off, including the concepts of satori and illusion.

🍂

Just how separate are illusion and satori anyway?

In reality, what we create illusions about and what we awaken to is one and the same thing.

🍂

Satori means that the buddha-dharma becomes reality.

The buddha-dharma is an interesting teaching because it says that all buddhas and all suffering beings are of the same nature. That's why it isn't buddha-dharma to imagine the buddhas as something over there on the other side.

🍂

Until we reach the place where there's no gap between us and buddha, the place where nothing special exists at all, we will suffer from hesitancy, fatigue and stagnation.

Where are you truly at home?

You have no traveling companions. Wherever you look, there's no one else! You've got to find the place you and you alone can reach.

"The great matter of lifelong practice comes to an end" means that the way of Buddha becomes reality; that it penetrates your flesh and bones.

Satori doesn't mean the end of illusion.

The buddha-dharma is ungraspable. To say that we have satori is going too far. To say that we don't have satori isn't going far enough.

Great satori means reality.

✿

You've got it backwards if you talk about stages of practice.
Practice is satori.

✿

Only zazen.

To ordinary people, this "only" doesn't seem like it's enough.
They want to get something in return for their practice.

✿

The word "only" is important. Just do it. For what? For
nothing! There isn't any tip—only doing.

✿

Satori is like a thief breaking into an empty house.

He breaks in but there's nothing to steal. No reason to flee.
No one who chases him. So there's nothing which could
satisfy him either.

✿

You really shouldn't show off with such a worn-out word as "satori."

❧

You talk about satori, but what you call satori is terribly small. The problem lies in your consciousness. Widen your consciousness a little and you'll realize that it's nothing.

❧

You can find satori everywhere in the world, like the air we breathe every day. We don't get satori in the future.

❧

Sometimes people beg me to certify their understanding of the dharma. As long as you have to ask others for their approval, you're not authentic. Still there are some who believe they've got satori because someone else gave them a certificate for it.

If you're already there, why ask others for directions?

❧

You've heard that wine makes people drunk, and now you're pretending you're drunk and believe that you've really drunk wine. That's just like some forms of satori.

Satori is becoming a technique. The buddha-dharma and mind of faith aren't techniques.

Satori isn't a chore; it means becoming natural.

16

To you who are impressed by scientific and cultural progress

Everyone is talking these days about progress, but I wonder where this progress is heading.

No animal is as dishonest as a human being. Humans eat their party snacks and dance in a circle; they do scientific research and drop hydrogen bombs on each other.

When you observe insects in a tank, you see how they bite into each other and hold on with all their might. It must be amusing to observe from another corner of the universe how humans stock up on atomic and hydrogen bombs.

Acting clever while at the same time being the biggest idiots—that's human fate.

People love it when things are complicated. Though things are complicated enough, even when we try to keep them as simple as possible, there are still some who make an effort to be especially complicated in everything they do.

The modern world musters up all of its knowledge just to run down a dead-end street.

People were idiots in the old days too. They wasted a fortune in gold and manpower building castles. What was it all for? To bicker with each other.

Today, people are even dumber. They build atomic and hydrogen bombs in order to erase humanity with one push of a button.

How is it that humanity itself, unlike its science, hasn't progressed in the least?

The Americans are only ordinary people, the Russians are ordinary people, the Chinese too are ordinary people—all ordinary people desperately competing with other ordinary people.

No matter how much dirt you pile up, it's still just dirt.

Science can build on the results of others, so it constantly makes progress. But humans can't build on the lives of others, so they make no progress. That's why everywhere we look we see helpless fools with deadly weapons—and that's dangerous!

An idiot sits at the computer, a dimwit in the cockpit of the jet and a madman at the control panel of the atomic rockets—that's the current problem.

In the buddha-dharma, we can't live on what others have left behind.

The reason science progresses is that it can build on what previous generations have left behind. In the buddha-dharma, it's just the opposite: it's to stop wanting to feed on what others have left behind.

Everyone is worried about humanity, but it's a matter of putting an end to what ordinary people call "humanity" and turning everyone into a buddha.

That which serves humans only leads them down a dead end.

People negotiate the market price of objects, but this market price isn't something you can rely on. Things whose market value can be disputed are just practical commodities. They're products.

Buddha isn't a product.

The Chinese character for "falsehood" (*itsuwari*) means "serving humans." Today, we consider culture and arts to be a service to humanity.

The world of culture and arts is constantly changing. Culture doesn't mean anything more than the further development of artifice. That's why culture is a tragedy.

What can we rely on no matter where we go? Only on life itself, which is unlimited in all directions.

When we carefully read Marx and Engels, we realize that the whole thing is just a matter of how we split up the loot.

Even if the whole of humanity were communist, until each and every one of us attains true freedom, we would still have this ceaseless bickering.

As long as each one of us isn't truly free, none of us can truly enjoy peace of mind.

17

To you who say you don't get along with others

Everyone talks about their own point of view, but who really cares? It'd be better if you just kept your mouth shut!

༄

Some say, "Who do you think I am anyway?" An ordinary person, what else?

Some are proud of their wealth, others of their name and position, still others of their satori. In this way they're just showing off how ordinary they are. People these days are so stupid!

༄

People always have something they can't forget. If they're rich, they can't forget their money. If they're intelligent, they can't forget their brains. If they're talented, they always think about how good they are at this or that. But whatever it is, it always gets in the way.

༄

It's only because we're so concerned about this sack of flesh that we think of ourselves as rich or beautiful or whatever. But when we die, everything is one. Nothing is yours anymore.

We're always trying to promote our ego. The only question is, how many years can we keep it up? When we're dead, our body is just a piece of meat.

The same moon sometimes seems to smile, and sometimes seems to cry. Sometimes we simply admire it over a glass of sake. But whichever moon people look at, they only see what corresponds to their karmic perception. None of that is real.

We're always trying to promote our ego. The only question is, how many years can we keep it up? When we're dead, our body is just a piece of meat.

Everybody reads the newspaper differently.

One person looks at the stock prices first, another reads the sports section first. One dives into the serialized novel, while another is mainly interested in politics. They differ so much because they're all lost in their own various consciousnesses. Only outside of these varying consciousnesses does the world that everyone shares reveal itself.

For this world hasn't been thought up by humans. It doesn't fit our personal viewpoints.

You say, "I saw it with my own eyes!" Nothing is as unreliable as your own eyes. They are just the eyes of an ordinary person.

You're fooling yourself if you think that the world as you see it is reality.

Everyone only sees what corresponds to their personal karmic perception. A cat sees differently than I do. And what about a bacillus, who weighs only a thousandth of a toilet fly, what does it think about? Certainly not the same things as I do. The bacillus and I have different perspectives on the world and on life.

The true world only appears when we have finished once and for all with all of these karmic views.

People's heads are all rigid. Every "ism" is a form of rigidity. This rigidity is the reason we don't recognize the buddha-dharma—no matter how close we are.

You cry out, "Peace, peace!" But if you would only be quiet, it would be so much more peaceful.

You say, "In my opinion…" But it's precisely when opinions and theories come into the picture that the bickering starts.

People let themselves be manipulated by the laws of their time when they believe that good and bad exist. In the past, blood feuds were legal, today they are illegal. In the past, adultery was illegal, today it's legal.

We believe that good and bad, pleasant and unpleasant, right and wrong all exist, that there are always two sides. But are there really two sides? No. Reality is only one—and even that "one" is empty.

People just need to be natural, but they try to squeeze even this naturalness into a framework. And because everyone has their own framework, they can never agree.

Everyone has their own consciousness. No one's consciousness is like anyone else's. It's completely individual and different.

⟨⟨⟩⟩

The "self" is nothing fixed.

If I hadn't by chance become a monk, then I probably wouldn't be talking about the buddha-dharma now. I'd probably be a gangster boss who wouldn't have anything more to say than, "And now I'll rip out your guts, you stinking dog!"

⟨⟨⟩⟩

Since the beginning of human history, this bickering has never stopped. The greatest wars have their origin in this bickering mind. War is simply the most exaggerated form of this.

⟨⟨⟩⟩

"Both you and me are just ordinary people." (*Prince Shōtoku, 17-Article Constitution*)

Since, in any case, it's just ordinary people who wage war on each other, everybody is wrong, friend as much as foe. The winner and the loser are in any case just ordinary people.

It's so sad to watch the world's conflicts. There's such a lack of common sense.

In the middle of a fight about irrigation it suddenly rains. Since the fight was only about the irrigation of their rice fields, the rain solves all problems.

A beautiful woman and an ugly woman: what's the difference when they're eighty?

Originally, everything is empty and clear.

– 18 –

To you who are complaining all the time that you haven't got any time

Everybody complains that they're so busy they haven't got any time. But why are they so busy? They only keep themselves busy to avoid boredom.

A person who practices zazen has time. When you practice zazen, you have more time than anyone else in the world.

If you aren't careful, you'll start making a big fuss just to feed yourself. You're constantly in a hurry, but why? Just to feed yourself.

Chickens too are in a hurry when they peck at their food. But why? Only to be eaten by humans.

How many illusions does a person create in their lifetime? It's impossible to calculate. Day in, day out, "I want this, I want that." A single stroll in the park is accompanied by 50,000. . . 100,000 illusions. So that's what it means to be "busy."

People are constantly out of breath—from running so quickly after their illusions.

You want to reach nirvana to be liberated from your present life? It is exactly that attitude which is called "transmigration."

The development of transportation has made the world smaller. Now we race around in cars, but where to anyway? To the pinball arcade! We step on the gas, just to kill time.

Some people spend the night playing mahjong only to swallow a handful of vitamins the next morning and hurry to work with swollen eyes.

In old kōans you often hear, "Where do you come from?" Here they're not asking for a place. Where do we all come from? Some desire sex. They come from sexual desire. Those who are greedy for money come from greed. "Please, give me a reference!" A person who says this comes from the desire for career and fame.

"I've got to do this, I've got to do that, I haven't got any time!" This is how some people go completely crazy. What should they do? The best thing would be nothing at all. They've just got to calm down.

Not carrying out any human activity—that's zazen.

Big businessmen and politicians complain that they're so busy. But at the same time they take their chances with two or three lovers. The question is simply, what is important to us?

There's no end to running away. There's no end to running after. In this moment, we practice zazen without complaints.

Nothing is more precious than a life lived out of the full-lotus posture.

Drifting in the world is like clouds drifting in non-mind. It isn't a matter of floating more quickly. Everything moves in non-mind.

Everything depends on interdependent origination; there is no substance.

It's the same with clouds: it's not that they exist, but they also don't not exist. At the same time, they do exist and they do not exist.

And now everybody's cracking their heads over that.

– 19 –

To you who are tumbling down the career ladder

When you're dead and you look back at your life, you'll see that none of this mattered in the least.

None of this matters at all. Stop blubbering! What a waste of tears.

Grow up a little and open your eyes. You'll see that you're making a great fuss over nothing.

Sometimes you hear actors in the theater saying, "But what should I do? What should I do?" This question has never occurred to me, because I just say to myself, "None of this really matters at all!"

Fortune and misfortune, good and bad—not everything is how it looks to your eyes. It's not how you *think* it is either. We've got to go beyond fortune and misfortune, good and bad.

The world that human beings know is only the world which they can glimpse through the peephole of their karmic delusions.

The real world appears before our eyes, once we stop staring at the world of our karmic delusions.

We have to break out of the world of delusion, rather than working our asses off in it.

You talk about your troubles and worries, but what do your troubles and worries really consist of?

Isn't it like someone who catches his own fart with his hand, smells it and bursts out saying, "Oh no, that really stinks!"

The more time you have, the more time you spend with your farts. At some point, you should get to know real suffering.

You want to hang or drown yourself in desperation? Come back down to earth and wake up to reality!

Suffering is nothing more than the suffering we create for ourselves. Some even take great pains to meticulously piece together their own suffering.

Because you relate everything to yourself, everything looks like a huge problem. Where there is no mind, there are no problems.

You suffer because you don't want to accept what has to be accepted.

Faith means the same thing as being beyond-thinking. It means acceptance.

You're worried about death? Don't worry—you'll die for sure.

20

To you who like to hear ghost stories

People often ask me if ghosts really exist. Somebody who racks their brains over something like that is what I call a ghost.

🍂

It's said that the dead appear as ghosts, but that's only true as long as you have the living. When the living are dead, they won't see any more ghosts.

🍂

Isn't everything a hallucination? It's only because we don't recognize this hallucination as a hallucination that we wander around in life and death.

🍂

Everyone is dreaming. The problem is simply the differences between the individual dreams.

🍂

When you are dreaming, it isn't clear to you that you're dreaming. If somebody hits you in the face, it hurts. But this pain is also only in the dream.

Some underpants are hanging to dry on a branch. Somebody sees them and thinks they've seen a ghost. Maybe you're thinking that something like that hardly ever happens in reality, but when we think, "I need money," "I want to become minister," "I want to get ahead"—aren't we all taking a pair of underpants for a ghost?

Everyone is talking about "reality," but this is only a dream. It's nothing more than the reality inside a dream.

When people are talking about revolution and war, we think that something really special is going on, but what is it besides struggling inside a dream?

When you die, you recognize your dream. Someone who doesn't put an end to dreaming before then is an ordinary person.

We can neither plan nor rehearse our dreams. In the same way, dharma is a dream, the teaching is a dream. A dream teaches a dream within a dream.

If somebody treats you to a meal within a dream, it's still just a dream. It doesn't have any calories.

◈

Wandering around inside your own illusions means living your life like a sleepwalker.

◈

Even if we put on a cool face, illusions are brewing in our heart of hearts.

◈

A year from now, think back to the illusions that you had yesterday during zazen:

Two bulls made out of mud have disappeared fighting into the sea.
No one has seen or heard from them since. (Tōzan Ryōkai)

21

To you who would like more money, love, status and fame

Heaven and earth give, air gives, water gives, plants give, animals give, humans give. All things give of themselves to each other.

It's only within this reciprocal giving that we can survive— regardless of whether we're thankful for it or not.

Nobody was granted life due to their personal merit. No one can live just by using their own strength. But nonetheless, we're all still only concerned with our own pocketbook.

Stupidity is being preoccupied with your own body. Wisdom is saying, "I am what I am, no matter how things end up."

A person outside of the way is someone who only thinks of gain and loss. A devil is someone who makes a profit off of this.

What a bore: making a long face and complaining about having no money, nothing to eat, and being stuck in debt. It's only because you believe that you are entitled to revel in life and always feel good that you moan and groan about your poverty.

Once during the war, I visited a coal mine. With the same outfit and headlamp as the miners, I got into the lift and down we went. At one point when we were going down it seemed to me as if suddenly we were going up again, but when I looked with the lamp at the wall of the shaft, I saw that we were still going down. In the beginning, when we were accelerating downwards, we could really feel that we were going downwards. Only when the velocity changed did it seem to us as if we were going up again.

In exactly the same way, when we think about our lives, we always go wrong when we mistake the fluctuating amounts for the final sum.

Saying you've had satori is just an interpretation of changing circumstances, as is saying you're lost in illusion. Saying "good" is an interpretation of change, saying "bad" is another. "Rich" is an interpretation, "poor" another.

It's self-evident that a poor man suffers less from his poverty than someone who was rich until a moment ago.

It looks like the poorest of the poor are left

Although you're really not so hungry, you say you've got nothing to eat. That alone makes you hungry. Words make for nightmares. Everyone makes a big deal over words.

I taught my parrot to say, "I'm doing fine!" One day the lamp fell and everything caught fire. Flapping his wings furiously, my parrot cried out his last words, "I'm doing fine, I'm doing fine!"—and died.

We're constantly being misled by our own body and mind, and we don't even realize it.

In the impermanent world we try to get forward with our name wherever we can. Yet aren't we all born naked? Only afterwards did we get our name, our jumpers and our nipple. Once we're big, we suddenly appeal to our importance, strength, intelligence or wealth just to make a name for ourselves. All along we're only naked.

What we construct as "the world" is nothing more than a mirage in the desert or a palace made out of ice. At another time, in another place, it would all melt away.

Everybody sleeps in the bed of buddha nature and only dreams their illusion.

Buddha says, "Everything is good as it is. There isn't a single lost being. There's no reason to get excited." But the lost beings cry out, "No! That's not how it is!"

Having the mind of the way means forgetting yourself for the others.

Forgetting the others for yourself means not having the mind of the way.

❦

Losing is awakening.

Winning is illusion.

❦

The difference between yourself and the others disappears only when you completely give yourself up for the others. That's what it means to save the others before you yourself are saved.

❦

Not coveting a single thing is the greatest gift you can give to the universe.

❦

The world in which everything is given freely offers a perspective which is cool and clear, wide and unlimited. This is completely different from the perspective in the world of "every man for himself."

Buddha's compassion is different from mere pity. His compassion provides a perch we can't fall from, no matter how we may stumble.

Big mind means buddha-mind. It means living twenty-four hours a day without grabbing onto a single thing. It means not hanging onto the conventions of the world.

– 22 –

To you who wish you could lead a happier life

You simply need to take a short break. Being buddha means taking a short break from being a human. Being buddha doesn't mean working your way up as a human.

In everything, people follow their feelings of joy, anger, sadness and comfort. But that's something different from the normal state of mind.

The normal state of mind means ceasefire. Without preferences, without animosity, without winning and losing, without good and evil, without joy and pain—that's everyday mind.

What do we have when we truly have a grip on things as they are? Beyond-thinking.

Beyond-thinking doesn't allow itself to be thought. No matter if you think so or not, things are simply as they are.

"All things are empty" means there's nothing we can collide with, because nothing is really happening. We only think something's happening because we are intoxicated by something.

❧

Nothing is ever happening, no matter what seems to be going on—that's the natural condition. Illusion means losing this natural condition.

Normally we don't recognize this natural condition. Normally we cover it with something else, so it's not natural anymore.

❧

The buddha-dharma means the normal condition. Yet in the world everything is unnatural. Domineering, succumbing and discussing everything to death are unnatural.

❧

What's important is not to win and not to lose—in triumph, not to lose the way, and in defeat, not to lose the way.

Yet people these days when they win, they lose their heads and lose the way, and when they lose, they lose it anyway. If they have money, they lose the way, and without money they lose it as well.

"If you do it like this, you'll get this result." That's how it works in the world, but not in the buddha-dharma.

"Taking care of people isn't about just any people. I myself have children at home. If I take care of them now, they can take care of me later." That's the logic of the world.

Simply doing what's good for nothing isn't so easy. Practicing it means dropping off body and mind, body and mind dropped off.

Crude things like getting in fights and picking up girls are obviously among the passions. However, the real problem isn't these, but much finer passions. We have to concentrate on the details.

"The mind is one with things as they are." Don't get stuck on anything, be open. Where no single thing has ever existed, no single thing should ever exist.

"Emptiness" means "each and every thing."

Every potato, no matter how small, has something to do with you. Every teacup concerns you.

True emptiness is the emptiness that cannot even be called "emptiness."

When you talk about heaven, you squeeze heaven into a frame.

True god is the god who has forgotten god; who has even stopped being god.

Offering that which fills the whole universe to everything in every instant, that's samadhi.

In Buddhist teaching, one isn't only one, being isn't only being, nothingness isn't only nothingness.

In Buddhist teaching, one is everything and everything is one. Being is nothingness and nothingness is being.

Someone asked a mathematician once if the number one really existed. The answer was that as a matter of fact, mathematics only operates on the assumption that the number one exists.

In Buddhism we don't even assume the existence of "one." It's said, "Two exists because of one, but don't hold onto this one either." One is everything, everything is one.

"As it is" means that there isn't the least confusion to be found anywhere in the entire universe.

Each place fills heaven and earth; every instant is eternal.

To practice the way of Buddha means to completely live out this present moment, which is our whole life, here and now.

Practice isn't something that you can pile up. Don't make it into a tool for anything either. Every aspect of daily life has got to be the practice of buddha.

It isn't good to wolf down your meal in order to practice zazen afterwards. We don't eat in order to work either. Just eat naturally. During your meal, just eat. Eating is practice.

Don't say strange things like, "the salvation of suffering beings" or "religious practice." Everything is all right as long as everything you do with your hands and feet is done with a solid comportment.

Recognizing impermanence means not grabbing at anything for yourself.

You speak loudly of "reality," but reality is nothing fixed. Everything is impermanent.

"Past mind cannot be grasped" means that the past is already past and doesn't exist anymore. "Present mind cannot be grasped" means that the present never stands still. "Future mind cannot be grasped" means that the future hasn't arrived yet.

In short, it all means impermanence.

What is the basis of formlessness?

There's nothing which isn't based on formlessness. But when we try to hold formlessness still, it becomes form. Formlessness means not running after and not running away.

Everybody is lost in delusion. People weep, laugh, are upset or happy, congratulate themselves or pout. When we stop this delusion, none of this remains.

To do this, we've got to massage our heads. We've got to be relaxed to be able to see things without delusion.

If your head has skin as thick as a grapefruit's, nothing can penetrate. If your head is as simple as a soldier's, you lack flexibility. Your head has got to encompass everything, the entire universe. That's the supreme way.

Even if we say that just practicing zazen is enough, we still have to eat when we're hungry, and when our money runs out, we've got to go begging. But if we're not careful, we'll make a routine out of that.

However good what we do is, as soon as it becomes routine, it isn't any good anymore. We mustn't hold on to anything. It's a matter of being free and unhindered.

Don't squeeze the way of Buddha into any frame.

A person who doesn't recognize differences is an idiot. A person who is constantly bothered by differences is an ordinary person.

A talent of mine is that I can always go back to being the errand boy named Saikichi, who I was when I was little.

Now, when I am about to leave on a trip and one more person comes with a pile of paper for me to fill with calligraphy, I can sometimes get a bit angry. But then I throw myself into it like in the days of Saikichi, the errand boy.

In those days, when I came home from a long day without any money and without any orders, I shook in fear of my hysterical stepmother waiting at home. As Saikichi, I was glad for every order, even when I had nothing in my belly.

To you who say that doctors and priests have it good

In the first year of the Meiji Era, the five-story pagoda of Hōryūji was up for sale for 50 yen, and it still found no potential buyers. Then, when they finally found somebody to buy the five-story pagoda of Kōfukuji for 30 yen, he only wanted to burn it down to gather up the gold afterwards. They told him, "If you do that, the whole town of Nara will go up in flames!" So he said, "Alright, to hell with it!" This is the only reason the pagoda has survived to this day.

The market value of things like these changes. There's nothing great about things whose market value change. We could also do without them. There are more important things. Zazen is what matters.

Outdated views: what adults teach children are often nothing more than outdated views. The view that good is good and bad is bad has already had its best days. Even a vegetable which was once good is inedible once it's past its prime.

We've got to always be able to see things from a fresh perspective. You say, "That's important," but what's important? There's nothing that's so important. When we die we've got to leave everything behind anyway.

The cultural goods and national treasures in Nara or Kyōto will sooner or later disappear, so we could actually set them on fire right now!

Recently there are temples in Kyōto that run hotels or boarding houses. It's strange how some people can't think of anything besides money and food.

Did Ryōkan leave money behind when he died or not? We're relieved to hear he didn't.

But in the world, people think differently. Here we can see that the way a monk thinks is completely the opposite of how the world thinks.

Today's priests haven't left their homes. They've simply moved from their straw-roofed huts into tile-roofed houses. Like a baker's son who has remodeled and now runs a crematorium.[14]

---

[14] Sawaki Rōshi often makes a stark contrast between "priest" (*bōzu, obōsan*) and "monk" (*sō* or *shukke*, literally "home-leaver"). He often characterizes priests by their preoccupation with the business of running a temple and making money. On the other hand, when he speaks of a monk, it is usually in the sense of a person who, in order to practice the way of Buddha, has left home (*shukke*), and all of the material benefits and preoccupations that go along with it.

During certain ceremonies, the master has to change his robes constantly. That's why somebody once said, "A priest isn't so different from a geisha!" Be careful, or you'll end up like that too.

A home-leaving monk means someone who completely lets go. It means letting go of group stupidity.

Today's priests only want to cling to things. That's why they're good for nothing.

When you feed a cat treats, it stops hunting mice, and a spoiled dog keeps no watch. Even humans aren't any good for work when they've got money and can take it easy.

For three hundred years, the Tokugawa policy was to control the priests with gluttony and warm robes so that they finally, like wild hogs that degenerate into ordinary pigs, lost their tusks and claws and allowed their marrow to be sucked out.[15]

---

15 During the Tokugawa Era (1600-1868), Buddhist temples benefited from a system that required that all Japanese families register at a temple and support it financially. Priests were also required to monitor and report on

Buddhists during the Tokugawa Era were completely happy to be yoked by Tokugawa policy. The fact that they didn't even consider themselves as religious is the reason for the current downfall of Buddhist teachings.

Today's priests are ashamed of their robes because of the distrust that they aroused after the suppression of Buddhism during the Meiji Era. The world laughs at these shady characters.

Today's priests are ashamed of being priests. In order to be recognized as little as possible, they only wear their robes when they go to do business, only as priests can they earn their living. That's their dilemma.

Catholic priests always wear their robes. They are proud to wear them. Now is that good or not?

---

these families to the government, particularly to ensure that they were not practicing Christianity, which was considered to be a threat to the government.

Later, in the early Meiji era, when such laws were abolished, there was a short period of backlash (1868-1874) where many expressed their very intense resentment of this oppressive system by destroying tens of thousands of temples.

It isn't easy to be a priest without making a business out of it. Yet a priest shouldn't really have anything to do with business.

A person has to set off fearlessly towards his own goal. A Buddhist has to have a clear attitude to life.

Every single day of your life in society is a test, and your whole life long you mustn't fail. That goes above all for the mind that saves suffering beings.

Even if you're only angry once, suffering beings won't come near you. Even if you're only greedy once, suffering beings will go away from you. This is where you've got to have a good handle on the way society thinks.

– 24 –

To you who say that priests run an easy business

It'd be funny if ghosts did their haunting whenever the priests botched a funeral. But even when the priests botch a funeral, the ghosts don't do anything. That's why the priest's life floats in limbo.

❧

Even a radio or a television doesn't transmit images or sound when it's not connected properly. Compared to this, priests are pretty sloppy. All I see are priests whose robes are a mess and don't even know how to sit zazen or go begging.

❧

Priests desperately try to get by through paying lip service to the Buddha's teaching, and lay people hope to get something out of it when they have priests pay lip service. How could this have anything to do with the Buddha's teaching, earning your living with memorized lip service?

❧

Today's priests say zazen isn't in demand anymore. They say, Sawaki is out of touch with the times.

❧

Buddhism has got to have access to something which neither communism nor democracy can easily disregard. It also has to have something that is capable of leading to where communism and democracy cannot.

If only all the decorations that Buddhists have piled up wouldn't get in the way so much.

Priests like to ask, "What will become of Buddhism in the future?" But who said that Buddhism is already at its end? Who says that Shakyamuni and Bodhidharma were idiots? Isn't it simply the priests who haven't any feeling for the way and who are idiots?

But since I can't really say that, I prefer to ask back, "How about your wife and your children, do they believe in you or not?"

A Zen monk is someone who leads a free life, centered around the way of Buddha.

Truly becoming a home-leaving monk involves recognizing the true self which can never be stained. It means creating your own life so that it fills the whole universe.

Tearing away all the Indian myths and all the Chinese myths and only practicing the naked content of the Buddha's teaching—that's leading a Zen life.

If we're not careful, spectators will pop up among religious people. When spectators appear, things aren't anymore like they should be. They turn religion into theater.

Asceticism is nothing more than the search for stimulation. The priests in the past were either seeking this stimulation or they were simply good-for-nothings. None of this has anything to do with religion.

Some people say, "I'm staying unmarried!" People wear so many different masks.

Magic tricks aren't wanted here. If we don't watch out, religion will become a magic show.

"No one else stands in the spot where you are." That means no spectators! Wherever spectators appear, it quickly becomes a sell-out.

Samadhi isn't a sell-out.

If priests aren't careful, they start putting on a show—and a bumbling burlesque show at that! There was a time when there were still stars who understood something about good acting, but today they're hardly to be found. Anyway, even when the stars are acting, they are still only actors.

When we lose sight of unsurpassable wisdom, we start comparing our abilities with other ordinary people. Simply have faith in unsurpassable wisdom.

You know what it means to be nothing special in the ordinary sense, but you've got to really understand that in the world of religion, those who are considered something special are nothing special.

What are your real motives? Sooner or later, you've got to honestly ask yourself this question. Don't you sometimes unconsciously make yourself into a performer who is only concerned with his show?

"Only you yourself can understand. Others cannot even manage to see it." (*Lotus Sutra*)

When it's about spectators, it's got nothing to do with the buddha-dharma.

Priests today want to do something for society, so they give money from the rich to the poor and play the merciful ones. This has nothing in the least to do with the buddha-dharma.

Buddha's teaching can only be practiced by yourself.

When organizations arise, it isn't religion anymore but business.

There is a certain sort of bad deed that is called "doing good."

When a throng of trainee monks in the main temples read half of the *Shōdōka* quickly and loudly, the pilgrims are overcome with awe. I've got no idea what's so awe-inspiring about that, but somehow everyone is overcome with awe.

These monks only gather together because they want to have their license, and the main temples do business by accumulating such monks. The same is true even for the temples in China. That's how they do business—without recognizing business as business.

The Buddha's teaching has declined these days because practice has declined. People just can't get it into their guts that practice itself is awakening.

Why is Japanese Buddhism worthless? Because in Japan you'll find the largest number of Buddhist treasures, just no practice. And where there's no practice, there's no buddha-dharma. Even if the seed of Buddha's teaching is there, it can't begin to function as long as it isn't cultivated with practice.

To you who want to study a little Buddhism to improve yourself

"Empty theories" is what we call it when bystanders play around with terminology.

✺

The buddha-dharma is nothing for spectators. It's about you.

✺

Religion doesn't mean changing the world around myself. It means changing my own eyes, my ears, my way of seeing and my head.

✺

The human body is set up in a very practical way, but what do we use this practical body for anyway? Usually, we use it as a slave to our illusions.

The buddha-dharma means using the body in a way that doesn't make it a slave to our illusions. That means putting body and mind in order.

✺

The buddha-dharma isn't an idea. It's about the problem, "How do I deal with myself?"

The way of Buddha means putting the absolute into practice, realizing it through practice.

The buddha-dharma means making a constant effort without getting anything for yourself. This is nothing that can be determined by asking, "What do I have to do?"

Nonetheless, you've got to do what you've got to do, and you mustn't do what you mustn't do. When you've got to give something, give even your own head. When you mustn't give anything, don't even give the tip of your tongue.

Practice isn't in things. It's in actions.

"Only a buddha together with a buddha is capable of penetrating this." (*Lotus Sutra*)

Only a cat understands the feelings of a cat. Only a buddha understands the buddha-dharma. Only a person who practices the buddha-dharma is a buddha.

Imagining a buddha without practicing the buddha-dharma has nothing to do with the buddha-dharma.

Religion is useless when it's paralyzed by concepts. Religion is life, and life has to keep moving.

You're stuck if you have nothing more to say than the mantra, "I take refuge in the *Lotus Sutra*." Life's got to be able to move in all directions: left and right, up and down. Don't turn into a mummy, don't let yourself dry out.

The whole world believes the practice of the Buddha way is about cutting off your illusions one by one, like dimming a lamp until all of a sudden it goes out.

But Mahayana practice is "vowing and working towards saving all suffering beings before saving myself." It's necessary to deliberately leave the illusions as they are in order to be of use to living beings.

This means we've got to be completely human. Being monotonously perfect isn't any good for anyone.

What has to be important in religion is how you live your life.

The buddha-dharma isn't some old legend like, "Once upon a time there was an old man and an old woman." It's not a fairy tale.

The buddha-dharma shouldn't be at all separate from your own problem. Separated from yourself, separated from this instant, there is no buddha-dharma.

The buddha-dharma doesn't lie in the distance. It isn't history either—it is you!

No social relationship, whether it's hierarchical or among equals, has anything to do with the buddha-dharma. Relationships like these aren't absolute. It's only because of ordinary feelings that we consider them real and rely on them.

Don't you see that the loved one you now hold in your arms will die? And even a millionaire will go when his time comes.

The old always talk about the good old days they miss so much, and young people always make fun of them. But what are young people really doing? They're saying, "Just wait until we grow up!" So, what both young and old are doing right now is only makeshift.

Humans laugh, cry, get angry, complain and suffer within all of their various relationships. "Drifting from one life to the next" means relying on these relationships and neglecting the present moment.

The description of the confusion within these relationships is what we call literature. Zazen, here and now, is free from these relationships. That's why Master Dōgen, who had nothing to do with all of this, doesn't make good material for novels.

Confusion reigns in the world because everyone uses their own ruler to measure what's big and small. Buddhism speaks of moving freely within big and small, narrow and wide.

Buddhism is immeasurable and limitless. If you're trying to understand Buddhism and aren't paying attention to this immeasurable limitlessness, you'll miss it completely.

– 26 –

*To you who like hearing something inspirational about
Buddhism*

Many say, "No matter how much Sawaki talks, his lectures
don't inspire me in the least!"

Obviously. That's because I myself am not "inspirational."
The buddha-dharma leads you to the place where nothing is
special.

They say, "When I hear Sawaki talk, my faith cools down."
Now I'm going to really put their faith on ice—this sort of
faith is nothing but superstition.

They say, "Sawaki's talks don't awaken any faith in me." They
don't awaken any superstition, that's all.

Whatever sutra you read, it's always about devoting your
body and life to the way. Why is it that the whole world
believes religion means praying to Buddha for good health
and good business?

However much good they do, everything that humans do is bad. If you give, all day long you think, "I gave!" If you do religious practice, you think, "I practiced, I practiced!" If you do something good, you never forget, "I did good, I did good!"

Does this mean that we should do something bad instead? No, even when we do good, it's bad. When we do something bad, it's even worse.

Beware of doing good.

A person who does good thinks they've done good. That's why they're worse than someone who has done something bad. Believe me, it's easier for those who do bad because they're humbled by it.

If you do good, you start to work yourself up about everything bad you suddenly see in others. When you have done something bad, you're quiet, because your own ass itches.

People don't only calculate when it's a matter of money. In everything they do they try to bargain up or down. That's because their body and mind haven't dropped off. Once body and mind have dropped off, all of this business stops.

Dropping off body and mind means immeasurability, limitlessness.

"The willow is green, the blossoms are red." Buddhist teaching is self-evident. But people cover it up with unnecessary categories: good, bad, useful, useless and so on.

Rather than simply sitting zazen, people try to put a melody on top of it. That's why they are able to sing their Buddhist hymns and somehow feel pious doing it.

"Do good, leave the bad." There's no doubt about that, but is it so clear what's good and what's bad? Good and bad go hand in hand.

Zazen goes past good and evil. It's not moral education.

If something like emptiness or nothingness "existed" then it wouldn't be emptiness or nothingness. The expression "seeing emptiness" means that there isn't even an emptiness to see.

As long as you don't get sick, you forget your body. Even I forgot my legs when they were still strong enough to walk and run. My legs only seem so important to me now because they're so weak. Whoever is healthy functions without being conscious of their own health.

It's the flaws that bother us. When no mental phenomena appear, there's nothing to worry about.

Buddhism must teach the liberation that has nothing to do with contracts and words. It is that which only a buddha and a buddha can confide to each other. If they don't both understand it together, it will never be understood at all.

To you who naively starts wondering about your true self

You can't hold on to your self. The very moment you give your self up, you realize the self which is one with the universe.

Precisely that self which I haven't thought up is who I really am.

The entire universe radiates the light of the self.

So, I fill the entire universe. I'm not that fool playing with his pocket change.

This body is the whole universe. If you don't have that kind of faith in yourself, you'll have a weak point you won't be able to hide. As soon as you get jealous or moody, you'll show it.

Faith means having faith that you are the entire universe, regardless of whether your intellect happens to find that convincing or not. Only this faith can support the religious effort that never tires.

⁂

Each one of us, whether we know it or not, has buddha nature. That means you are included in all things, manifesting the true form of reality.

⁂

The form of reality lies open before you. Doubting this is wasted effort.

⁂

To study the Buddha way means to study the self which isn't twisted and can't be misled.

⁂

Just forget everything you've picked up since you were born.

⁂

What's called "dropping off body and mind" doesn't mean anything more than simply to stop insisting on "I", "me" and "mine."

In *Gakudōyōjinshū* it is written, "Having awakened mind means seeing impermanence." And the *Vairocana Sutra* says, "Awakening means directly seeing how your own mind really is." That means above all that seeing impermanence is truly seeing your self.

The expression "non-self" doesn't mean being an idiot. It means being one with the universe.

The other side of non-self is that all things are true and real.

Non-self, non-mind doesn't mean drifting away aimlessly in unconsciousness.

Non-self means not going against what is necessary. It means obeying the order of the universe by functioning along with the universe.

Is life inside of time? No, it's the other way around: time is inside of life.

And there's no life outside of your practice.

When a drop of water enters the sea, and when a speck of dust settles on the ground, then that drop is already the sea, and that speck of dust is already the earth.

When the flood of religious ideas reaches its culmination, they arrive at the point which Buddhism calls "the self that fills the entire universe."

All things are contained in my self. That's why, in my actions, I also have to pay attention to what others think.

The Buddha way shouldn't be unaware of society.

The buddha-dharma and the human point of view look at each other directly in the eyes. This is what's meant by the two truths of reality and the world.

Deluded living beings are the Buddha's best clients. That's why the buddha-dharma has to be very careful on this point.

It is because we are grateful towards society that whenever we use something, we think of those who will need it after us.

If you have "mind," you always have something to complain about. If you have "no mind," you have no mind of compassion either.

Don't have either mind or non-mind. That's difficult. That means thinking from the depths of non-thinking.

What's called "beyond thinking" is something so vast that it can entirely contain mind as well as non-mind.

Buddha doesn't have a fixed form. That's why we can't measure him.

When you ask what Buddhism is, the answers are "studying the Buddha way means studying the self" (*Shōbōgenzō Genjōkōan*) and "truly recognizing your own mind" (*Vairocana Sutra*).

So, when you ask why we begin religious practice, the answer has to be that we are finally setting off on the journey in search of our self.

But if you're not careful, it might be that you'll spend your whole life running around like a ghost, without knowing what you're searching for or why.

Step forth in your practice, walking in your straw sandals, getting blisters in search of the one thing without personal nature, without profit. This practice isn't something outside. It's turning the light inwards, towards the inside of the self.

You hear about the dharma gate of peace and happiness, but this peace and happiness isn't how the world understands it. Finishing once and for all with that worldly peace and happiness is true peace and happiness.

The buddha-dharma doesn't lie in the distance, but we can't expect to get it for free either. It means becoming clear about yourself.

– 28 –

To you who thinks Buddhism is the greatest idea in human history

Ideas are based on how things would stand if everything were already settled. The buddha-dharma is about that which hasn't settled yet. Things are still in motion.

Religion isn't an idea. It's practice.

What an experiment is for scientists is what real practice is for us. In the same way that science is meaningless without experiments, Buddhism is meaningless without practice.

Don't get lost in thoughts about the buddha-dharma.

Be careful that you don't handle the buddha-dharma like canned goods which have nothing to do with reality.

Your explanations and your anecdotes are foolish like everything that comes out of your mouth. The expression on your face has already said how it really is.

⟜

The buddha-dharma isn't set in books. No matter how many sutras are piled up in the library, without human beings they're worthless. It's something that takes place between human beings. That's why we say, "buddha-dharma is practice."

⟜

The content of terms and ideas changes every instant. Nothing is fixed.

That's why in the *Hannya Shingyō* it says that eye, ear, nose, tongue, body and mind do not exist and that all phenomena and the entire process of perception are empty.

Wherever you look, no two things are the same. Each one of us has his own face.

⟜

"Form is emptiness, emptiness is form." When you put it into words you impose a sequence onto it. When you say it aloud, one comes after the other. In reality it's simultaneous. "In reality" means in the practice.

You can express reality completely freely with words. Yet these words are not in themselves reality.

If reality were in the words themselves, we would burn our tongue whenever we said "fire," and whenever we talked about wine, we would get drunk. In reality, it isn't so easy.

When reality lies before us, words are superfluous. Words without reality are empty theories.

When we've seized the content, we can freely use words or not as we like.

A person who can't say it with simple words hasn't thoroughly digested what he's learned.

Professors of Buddhism spend their whole life calculating the number of provisory teachings, without ever getting even a bit of the truth in their stomach. They think learning how to count small change is the same as becoming rich.

The Indians love counting everything exactly. They can tell you the exact number for anything: the exact number of different ways to pick your nose, different ways to fart and so on.

Professors of Buddhism look at Buddhism as reference material, not as an expression of their self.

You've got to be clear that it makes a huge difference whether you're completely ready to accept something or not. That's true for every precept, for every sutra, every thought and for every culture. In every situation, that's how it is. That goes for your life as a whole as well.

There's nothing more phony than teaching Buddhism without any real practice.

However, when you see the sutras as a symbolic expression of the practice, then there's no art form that's quieter and more transparent.

The transmission takes place outside of the sutras without relying on words. That's why there isn't any buddha-dharma to be found in the sutras.

Does that mean that the entire body of sutras is nothing but lies? Not at all. All sutras are true—when you read them with true eyes.

Sugar is sweet, even if it doesn't say anything. It doesn't say, "Believe me, I'm so sweet." In the same way, if we say "sugar" with the mouth, it doesn't taste sweet. Only when it touches the tongue is it sweet. Sugar isn't a word.

Does that mean that words have no meaning? Not at all. I just need to say, "Bring me the sugar!" and you'd bring me some, wouldn't you?

Buddhism is difficult because it teaches something that can't be explained.

Nothing that you've understood and learned by rote is Buddhism.

Old people justify their old habits with their old experiences.

True wisdom is that which doesn't have to change when everything else changes.

When the second ancestor, Master Eka, visited the first ancestor, Master Bodhidharma, he wasn't allowed to enter. It was a snowy night on the ninth of December when he waited for dawn outside the entrance. In the old texts it's written, "The snow reached his hips. The cold went to the bone."

Bodhidharma spoke without looking at him, "Someone who is as conceited and superficial as you shouldn't ask about the true teaching so light-heartedly." Snowed-in to the hips, frozen to the bone, you could hardly call him conceited and superficial. Or could you?

Then Eka cut off his left arm and held it out to Bodhidharma. It's written that Bodhidharma let him in with the words, "All buddhas completely forgot the world of forms when they set off on the way for the first time. You, who cut off your arm before me, can seek something here."

After the second ancestor cut off his arm, he must have lost a lot of blood. I'm afraid to ask whether the wound was at least bandaged before the dialogue took place.

People in the world understand at best that hardships can improve them. But the second ancestor submitted himself so completely to Bodhidharma that he even cut off his arm while standing in the snow. What did it do for him? In the end he was betrayed by persecutors of Buddhism and murdered. Not exactly what people hope for.

To you who are pleased when someone compliments the depth of your faith

Many confuse faith with a type of intoxication. Faith means, however, just the opposite—complete sobriety from any form of intoxication.

When most people in the world talk about the mind of faith, they don't think it's anything more than kissing up to Buddha.

"Do what you like with the others, but at least give me a first-class ticket to paradise!" Prayers like that have got nothing to do with the mind of faith.

Faith means clarity and purity. The mind of faith means truly becoming clear about your own mind.

Faith means being clear and pure. It means being at ease. But some people misunderstand this as well and think faith is about getting worked up. So, they try with all their might to do so, until they realize that it's not so easy to get truly worked up. Then they just act as if they were.

✿

Everyone wants to go to paradise, but have you ever really seen it? If you think you have, you must have been mistaken.

✿

There are people who want to live as long as possible. Any religion that offers it will do. What they have to believe in doesn't matter at all. That's how they waste their lives away.

✿

When some new religious group starts picking up huge numbers of followers, suddenly everybody thinks there must be something true about it.

✿

The number of followers doesn't determine if a religion is good.

If it were simply a matter of who had the largest numbers, doesn't the club of ordinary people have the most members? No, it's the bacteria—there's even more of them!

✿

Aren't a huge pile of crazy ideas dumped on us humans, ideas that go by the names of "faith," "satori" and so on?

Faith doesn't mean praying for good health, good business, harmony in the family and well-being for your children.

Faith means pure clarity, the pure clarity in which the mud settles and the excitement calms. It means nothing besides completely coming to your senses.

Faith isn't something secondhand. Buddha isn't something secondhand. If it's not about your problem here and now, it's got nothing to do with faith.

"Let's put it off until later." You can't dismiss the problem like this. The question is whether you, here and now, truly can see Buddha's body and hear his teaching.

The way isn't about asking others. It's about returning to your self.

Some call Buddha's name as if they wanted to flatter him with their faithful hearts. Others believe that they practice zazen in order to get satori. As long as it's only revolving around you as an individual, it's got nothing to do with the buddha-dharma.

Your little personal problems aren't interesting. The universal whole is the problem here. No matter how big your satori is or how important, charitable or good you are, if it doesn't concern anything besides you as an individual, it's merely a scene in the play of self-deception.

– 30 –

To you who say that the Shōbōgenzō *is difficult to understand*

Because you want to understand Buddhist teaching from the standpoint of human thought, you are going 180 degrees in the wrong direction.

Master Dōgen doesn't expect anything from us that's not humanly possible. It's simply a matter of becoming natural, without empty thoughts or peculiarities. Buddhism in general doesn't demand anything special from us, only that we become natural.

Some verses in the sutras might seem special to us, for example, "The white hair between his eyebrows illuminates the 3,000 worlds." But that's only a literary symbol for the samadhi that is the king of all samadhis.

Master Dōgen's whole life was one uncompromising, penetrating inquiry into himself.

There's no buddha outside of practice, and no teaching except for beyond-thinking. Those are Master Dōgen's essential principles.

Beyond-thinking means that the excitement of illusion and awakening quiets down.

"Studying the Buddha way means studying yourself. Studying yourself means forgetting yourself. Forgetting yourself means being certified by the 10,000 things." (*Shōbōgenzō Genjōkōan*)

That means that I become buddha, together with all others.

Something that is fascinating about Master Dōgen is how he saw the buddha-dharma as the self, and didn't think that Buddhism was just fairytales for ordinary people. In the same way, spreading the buddha-dharma is the practice of zazen itself, not building temple halls or pagodas.

Master Dōgen's zazen is a completely transparent zazen. It's of no use to ordinary people.

"Don't practice the buddha-dharma for yourself. Don't practice to make a name for yourself. Don't practice to profit from it. Don't practice to have spiritual experiences. Only practice the buddha-dharma for the sake of the buddha-dharma." (*Gakudōyōjinshū*)

That's his buddha-dharma.

Master Dōgen "returned with empty hands." When he came back from Japan, he didn't show off some satori the way others show off their tattoos. The story of his emptyhanded return completely relaxes our grasping onto any sort of fixed idea like achieving satori through zazen.

In our religion, awakening has existed since the eternal past. We only need to put it into practice.

"When your body is rooted in this original, authentic awakening, the practice which cannot be thought flows naturally from the body." (*Shōbōgenzō Bendōwa*)

When you eat your rice, your belly fills up, right? That's exactly what's meant by "practice and certification are one." If you stuff yourself once, that doesn't mean that you'll never need to eat again. You've got to eat every day, your whole life long.

In exactly the same way, you've got to continue with the practice your whole life long.

If you are so concentrated on your kōan that no single thought bothers you anymore, that only means that you've pushed your bothersome thoughts aside for a minute. Dōgen Zenji's practice of *shikantaza* is about something much broader. It's about viewing the entire landscape of the self.

The fact that the zazen of the buddhas and ancestors has been authentically transmitted means that none of us have thought it up all by ourselves. Transmission doesn't mean some sort of goods have been transported.

"Saving the others before saving myself" is ultimate selflessness. I forget myself, and the separation between myself and all suffering beings dissolves.

The expression "awakening the mind" means saving the others before saving yourself.

"Saving the others before saving myself" means that you and all suffering beings on this great Earth attain the way simultaneously. It means experiencing through your own body that mountains and rivers, grass and trees and the lands of the Earth all are buddha nature.

In other words it means returning home.

In *Zazen Yōjinki* it is written, "Zazen is like sitting peacefully after returning home."

Returning home exhausted and sitting peacefully, that's zazen—but not only zazen. Master Dōgen teaches that the person who does zazen also eats and cooks. His *Tenzō Kyōkun* follows from this spirit.

The *Eihei Shingi* talks about how we put our hands and feet in order; how we put our life in order.

But you still have researchers who cry out, "In the *Eihei Shingi* we have stumbled upon very interesting primary texts!"[16]

---

[16]   The *Eihei Shingi* is a collection of texts by Dōgen Zenji concerning various aspects of practice in a monastery, such as preparing, serving and receiving meals; sleeping and waking up; working and living together, and of course zazen practice.

Master Dōgen doesn't teach any unshakable peace of mind, but rather unshakable peace of body.

The buddha-dharma is how we behave. Our behavior must become the buddha-dharma. When the Buddha was still alive, everyone comported themselves correctly.

Master Dōgen doesn't teach any unshakable peace of mind, but rather unshakeable peace of body.

No fish says, "I've swum through all the waters." And no bird says, "I've already flown through all the skies." Nonetheless, the fish swims in the whole ocean, and the bird flies in the whole sky. Herrings no less then whales swim in the whole water.

It isn't quantity, but rather quality which is the issue here. Our hands and feet don't have more than a square meter for their range of activity. Nonetheless, we affect the whole universe.

They say that when the golden phoenix beats his wings, the waters of the seas are emptied and the dragons at the bottom of the sea are exposed. So the phoenix can grab them and gobble them up.

But even this phoenix will never fly through the entire sky, and at the same time even a sparrow flies within the entire sky. This is the realized *kōan*: living here and now in endless space and limitless time.

❧

"A thousand sutras and ten thousand attainments cannot equal a single realization." (*Shōbōgenzō Den-e*)

The buddha-dharma is above all realization—the real thing.

❧

A Christian asked me once, "My priest has said that no religion has spread so many lies as Buddhism. Is that really true?"

I answered, "Now you've hit the nail right on the head, my friend!"

The *Lotus Sutra* as well as the *Garland Sutra* and the *Shōbōgenzō* are nothing but lies, when they're not put into practice. Without zazen, Buddhism is a total lie.

❧

"The one great matter of my lifelong search has been settled here." (*Shōbōgenzō Bendōwa*)

That's nothing especially fantastic. For each of us, the one great matter of our lifelong search is already settled. No one is missing anything. We aren't at all different from Shakyamuni.

Thinking you are foolish is the most foolish thing in the world.

According to Dōgen Zenji it doesn't matter at all whether we are awakened or not. "Eyes horizontal, nose vertical." There isn't much more to a person, awakened or not.

Somebody once called Master Dōgen "incomplete," but was this person himself complete?

Something completed isn't necessarily better. Finished products aren't worth a bit more.

From time to time it may seem to us as if good and evil were something settled.

Dōgen Zenji says, "Good and bad is time. Time is neither good nor bad" (*Shōbōgenzō Shoakumakusa*). We've got to begin at the place where neither good nor bad exist.

Dōgen Zenji says, "When you recognize the danger in the world, for you there is no more danger in the world."

There isn't any career to be made in the monk's life. Whoever tries to make a career as a monk has left home for nothing.

No one has ever rejected the search for fame as much as Master Dōgen.

– 31 –

*To you who say that Buddhism doesn't have
anything to do with you*

In prison, the prisoners puff themselves up in front of the
guards and say, "Take a good look at yourselves. Without us
you wouldn't have anything to eat!"

That's exactly how it is with us ordinary people. Because we
exist, the buddhas exist. Without us ordinary people, the
buddhas would have been out of work long ago.

In this sense, ordinary people and buddhas aren't separate
beings but stand in interrelation to each other.

A bodhisattva is someone who awakens suffering beings.
He's an ordinary person who has what Buddha's aiming at
clearly and decidedly in sight.

A bodhisattva is an ordinary person seeking the way.

Being a bodhisattva means daring to go astray in the midst of awakening. Don't say, "I'm awakened. The ordinary people should see for themselves how to get out of their illusion."

It is because in bodhisattva practice we dare to go astray together with the ordinary people that this practice is of immeasurable length and unlimited breadth.

"Awakening the mind" means "saving the others before I save myself." That means that I mustn't be the least bit different from all the other suffering beings.

When you talk about Buddha, you're thinking of something far away that's got nothing to do with you, and that's why you're only running around in circles.

If Buddha were just a buddha for himself somewhere over there, then that wouldn't have anything to do with being a buddha.

Buddha is a buddha precisely because he stands in relation to suffering beings.

If there is supposed to be some god outside of myself, then that is a heretical teaching of god and self. You yourself have to be god.

If the god who created all things is supposed to exist somewhere else, then it's got nothing to do with the buddha-dharma.

We don't become buddha through zazen. We were already buddha before we began with zazen. It isn't anything more than our dream when this buddha gets upset, cries or sleeps.

Ordinary people are dragged around by their karmic conditioning. Looking at the world from the standpoint of their conditioned feelings and getting on each other's nerves, they continue being dragged from one life to the next, from one world to the next. This is what's called "transmigration."

That's why there isn't anything else left to do besides right now, in the midst of this karmic conditioning, freeing ourselves from this karma.

When we remove for a moment the spectacles of our conditioned feelings, we recognize what Shakyamuni Buddha said upon his awakening: "The great Earth and all its living beings attain the way in this very moment. Mountains and rivers, grasses and trees are without exception buddha nature."

That means that, in Shakyamuni's eyes not a single one of us is in illusion. We, all suffering beings, are the ones who insist so stubbornly on our illusions. Shakyamuni's compassion and the Buddha's teaching consist in awakening us to this fact.

Ordinary people are tricky characters. Sometimes they're like hungry ghosts, animals or demons, with all kinds of quirks stuck to them. In the end they're nothing more than a pile of quirks.

In the old days there were all sorts of supernatural events, but in today's neon light, ghosts just don't appear anymore. They haven't got any place to hide.

However, the real ghosts and ghouls, whose karmic wandering goes back into the darkness of beginningless time, are those who believe in their "I." The number of those ghosts hasn't decreased in the least.

Ordinary people and buddhas have the same form.

Awakening and illusion have the same form.

Omniscience means knowing that your buddha nature doesn't have any cracks you could fall through.

The night train carries you even while you sleep.

The buddhas of the three worlds carry us suffering beings on their shoulders. That's why they are constantly in the realm of illusion.

All suffering beings are saved by the buddhas of the three worlds. That's why they are constantly in the realm of awakening.

In "The Life Span of the Tathagata" chapter of the *Lotus Sutra,* it's written, "Since I have reached buddhahood, uncountable millions and billions of eons have passed."

That's not only the case for Shakyamuni. It's also true for Kōdō Sawaki and for everyone else as well. Since the achievement of buddhahood, endless eons have passed. That's what the *Lotus Sutra* says. Being a buddha for eons isn't Shakyamuni's exclusive privilege.

That's why we don't practice now in order to attain some satori later on. We don't practice, running after some private satori. By nature, we have always, eternally been true buddhas.

Zazen doesn't mean anything besides putting Buddha's practice into practice. That's why we speak of "practicing buddha."

When we practice the buddha-dharma, we are buddha. Or better yet, it is precisely because we are buddha already that we can practice the buddha-dharma.

If you asked me who Shakyamuni was, rather than saying that he's like white paper, I'd say he's like the blue sky—perfectly transparent and seamlessly connected to all suffering beings everywhere.

Buddha has to be connected to all suffering beings. If someone loses his child, Buddha has to shed tears with him. It's cowardly to claim that you are staying free from group stupidity just in order to avoid contact with people.

What a shopkeeper does out of greed, a Buddhist does out of compassion. That's why you've got to be thoroughly familiar with the rules of the world.

You believe that Buddhism is a little different from everything else. But it's not like that at all—Buddhism is each and every thing.

"Each and every thing is my child." That's how the buddhadharma sees the world.

When adults are only adults, children don't grow up. When children cry, you've got to cry with them. Adults have to be children, children have to be adults.

Between buddhas and ordinary people, the buddha-dharma and the social world, satori and illusion, ascending and descending, wisdom and compassion—there's got to be a lively exchange among all of these.

No one's asking you to become a gourmand or to constantly climb the career ladder. But if you are too stupid to understand people's appetite for delicacies or their ambition to have a career, then something in you isn't right.

It isn't enough just to step up to the world of equality. You have to step down into the world of difference too.

What's called "old mind" is compassionate mind or parental mind; and this mind completely contradicts every theory.

Parental mind is full of contradictions. Like when a parent says, "Get out and stay out! And don't eat any blowfish, dear—it's poisonous."

The paper screen is so cold when there's no child to rip a hole in it anymore.

To you who say that your body, just as it is, is already Buddha

Ishikawa Goemon said, "Even once I have disappeared and all sand has washed into the sea, the seeds of thievery in the world will never be exhausted."[17] This is how he sings the praises of that "thief-nature" that penetrates heaven and earth. However, as long as we don't act like Goemon we won't become thieves.

It's also said that all things have buddha nature, and that it completely penetrates heaven and earth. But as long as we don't act like a buddha, we don't become buddhas.

When you, inseparable from Buddha, put Buddha's activity into practice, only then are you a buddha. When you act like a fool, then you're a fool.

It's only in your approach to life that Buddha appears.

---

[17]   This was said just before he was executed. See footnote on page 36.

Some say, "This mind is Buddha. That means that when I think that I'm Buddha, then I'm Buddha." Have you ever heard such nonsense?

You can say that a match contains fire, but if I don't know that I have to strike the match, and if I don't actually do so, I won't have any fire. You can't say that the match itself is fire.

"If it is not put into practice, it doesn't appear. If it is not certified, you cannot receive it." (*Shōbōgenzō Bendōwa*). Practice is realization.

Even if I had a gas stove here, as long as I didn't light it with a match it wouldn't warm up. Even if we say that everyone already has buddha nature, this "has" by itself doesn't help us at all. We have to light the fire of buddha nature.

A long time ago, a believer approached the monk Gakushin and asked him, "At the moment, I don't feel like calling Buddha's name. Wouldn't it be better if I waited until I felt the urge to do so?"

Gakushin's answer was, "When a good-for-nothing like you holds off calling Buddha's name until he feels like it, he could wait his whole life. Whether you feel like it or not, just call out Buddha's name!"

And he added a poem to this:

Only when you pull on the cord in the deep autumn fog with all of your heart
does the bell sound in the rice paddy on the mountain.[18]

The Buddha way means practice.

Buddha statues and paintings aren't buddhas. When we present buddha statues and paintings as buddhas, we promote idolatry.

In Buddhism, the formless posture of each individual thing is Buddha. My formless posture, my zazen and my *kesa*[19] are Buddha. Just eating meals, just working, just cooking—that's Buddha.

The expression "constant effort without profit" means throwing your entire body and mind into the Buddha's teaching.

Not yearning for anything, not running away from anything —that's constant effort without profit.

---

[18] A poem by Gakushin, a Jōdō priest (1722-1789).
[19] The *kesa* is the Buddha's robe, transmitted to a monk upon ordination.

"Movement is Zen, sitting is Zen. In speaking, silence, work and rest, the body finds peace." (*Shōdōka*)

Because a buddha says it, it's the truth. But when an ordinary person says it about himself, it leads to disastrous misunderstandings.

"Illusion is awakening, ordinary people are buddhas."

You might think this means "with my body as it is," but it isn't like that. An ordinary person, with his body as it is, in the end, is nothing more than an ordinary person.

Correct would be: the body in which an ordinary person forgets the ordinary person is, as it is, Buddha.

Only when you look at the world from the point of view of the Buddha way will it appear as the Buddha way.

Practicing the Buddha way doesn't mean stirring up your karmic feelings. It means being accepted by the buddhas as an equal.

We've got to understand what time and space is for a buddha. It isn't how an ordinary person sees and hears things. It doesn't fit into an ordinary person's scheme of things.

⁂

If you don't ever take a fresh look at the human side of things from this completely different point of view, you can't possibly understand.

⁂

Any buddha that humans have thought up isn't a buddha.

⁂

When we say Buddha is unlimited, it means that he's beyond any fixed form. It isn't a measurement of his size.

⁂

Buddha is sharp-witted, cheerful and free of attachment. Nevertheless, lots of people these days think that Buddha is dreary and ominous.

⁂

Samadhi means the pure clarity of your own nature. It is that which transparently binds ordinary people with Buddha.

In "beyond-thinking" there are neither ordinary people nor buddhas.

Beyond-thinking is true practice and true activity. Zazen is beyond-thinking put into practice.

Any remaining doubts we might have are secretly swallowed by beyond-thinking, by the buddha-dharma.

Yet, for ordinary people the buddha-dharma is still unsatisfying. It doesn't satisfy ordinary people's needs.

Because it is an ordinary person who's practicing the Buddha way and doing zazen, naturally it isn't pure.

Nonetheless, it's like "the heron who does not change the taste of the water it drinks, and like the bees who do not harm the smell of the flowers they visit." (*Eiheikōroku*)

In the same way, the merits of zazen are perfected without an ordinary person being able to harm zazen in the least.

Some think following the buddha-dharma is to start out as ordinary people, and then follow some moral plan to improve themselves. How foolish! The first principle of the buddha-dharma says that we are all buddhas.

However, if someone has never aroused the mind of awakening, how could we say that his "mind is, as it is, Buddha"? (*Flower Ornament Sutra*)

– 33 –

To you who are going out of your mind trying so hard to attain peace of mind

The buddha-dharma is immeasurable and unlimited. How could it ever have been made to fit into your categories?

In any case, only things for ordinary people can be grasped. Grasping for money, clinging to health, being attached to position and title, grasping for satori—everything you grasp only becomes the property of an ordinary person.

Letting go of the possessions of ordinary people—that's what it means to be a buddha.

When peace of mind only means your personal satisfaction, then it's got nothing to do with the buddha-dharma.

The buddha-dharma teaches limitlessness. That which is measureless has to be accepted without complaint.

The buddha-dharma is of limitless breadth. But when you try to hold it still, you've lost it.

We're not talking here about dried cod. Living fish have no fixed form.

⁂

When you try to grasp the buddha-dharma, you only end up constipated.

⁂

"Only a buddha and a buddha can penetrate it completely." (*Lotus Sutra*) A person who isn't a buddha himself can't accept the buddha-dharma.

⁂

You lack peace of mind because you're running after an idea of total peace of mind. That's backwards.

Be attentive to your mind in each moment, no matter how unpeaceful it might seem to be. Great peace of mind is realized only through practicing within this unpeaceful mind. It arises out of the interplay between peaceful and unpeaceful mind.

⁂

A peace of mind that is totally at peace would be nothing more than something readymade. Real peace of mind only exists within unpeaceful mind.

⚜

When dissatisfaction is finally accepted as dissatisfaction, peace of mind reigns.

It's the mind of a person who was deaf to criticism when he finally listens to others talking about his mistakes.

It's the mind of a person who was naked and begging for his life, when he suddenly dies peacefully.

It's the mind of a person who has suddenly lost the beggar who had been pulling at his sleeve, following him around everywhere.

It's the mind after the flood, once the makeup of piety has washed away.

⚜

There isn't any world in which everything's right. Nonetheless, everyone is wandering around in search of it. What good does it do to wander around endlessly or to cry yourself to sleep in desperation?

That's backwards. It's a matter of sitting immovably in the world and not wandering around.

Peace of mind means not running after anything.

Words like "arriving" or "satori" shouldn't refer to intellectual understanding. They mean being unmoved, no matter what happens. In life and in death.

Many believe peace of mind means freeing themselves from suffering in order to always be happy. That's mistaken. However great our suffering may be, the answer isn't to thrash around with your hands and feet. It's to stay calm.

If you want to observe the state of a person who doesn't have any peace of mind, look at a mouse in a trap. It thrashes around with all of its might. Then a man sees it and throws it to the cat who happily eats it. This is how you can understand that thrashing around with your hands and feet is a waste of energy.

Instead, sit peacefully in zazen.

How could a human being ever have peace of mind? The real question is what you're doing with this human life. What you're doing with this stinking sack of flesh—that's the issue.

In the buddha-dharma, the ordinary person and Buddha aren't two different creatures.

Peace of mind isn't about sitting there like a bump on a log.

The buddha-dharma is realized through practice; it's put into effect by the body. That means that zazen is all about the correct tension and placement of muscles and ligaments.

Practice means to practice an approach to life with zazen as the measure.

Wherever this practice is found, peace of mind is fully actualized. The practice is our comportment in every aspect of our lives.

Only when you pull on the cord in the deep autumn fog with all of your heart

does the bell sound in the rice paddy on the mountain.[20]

---

20   See footnote 18, page 189.

To you who are aiming at the ultimate way of life

It has to be as it is, but it can be any which way.

Nothing has to be done in any particular way, yet it has to be done in the highest and best possible way.

Sen no Rikyū[21] once hired a carpenter to drive a nail into a pillar. After considering it thoroughly, he decided on the exact point. The carpenter made a little mark and then took a break. When he finally got around to actually hammering the nail in, he couldn't find his mark anymore. Sen no Rikyū reconsidered the matter and eventually called out, "Here, here's a good place!" When they looked at it closely, it was clear that it was exactly the same spot where the carpenter had made his mark before.

In the middle of pure formlessness, there is an ultimate direction. In the same way, there is an ultimate facial expression among a person's many facial expressions.

---

[21] Considered the founder of the Japanese tea ceremony.

What's called "having magical powers" doesn't mean anything more than having a facial expression that isn't muddled.

❧

We think that we're constantly misled by our deluded feelings and that nothing can be done about it. We think that there's a push and pull between the Buddha's teaching and our foolish feelings. But that's backwards.

The buddha-dharma says that we aren't at all different from Buddha. All things manifest the truth. What you learn in the buddha-dharma are the basics of practice.

❧

Practice means asking with your whole being the question, "What can I do right now for the Buddha way?"

❧

It's a matter of seeing what's above and below and what's to the left and right, without losing sight of here and now.

❧

Everything we do involves everything, even to the last reaches of the universe.

This moment is eternal. This is what we have to devote ourselves to wholeheartedly.

How should I face this situation? Our efforts revolve around
this point.

Giving has got to have a direction too. You shouldn't give a
robber your keys and a pistol. You need courage as well as
wisdom when you give.

Deeply studying the impermanence of all things means
deeply studying every single instant, without losing sight of
your direction.

"What does this situation require?" Devoting yourself to
each and every situation of your whole life in this way is the
meaning of deeply studying impermanence. Impermanence
doesn't just mean that all of us will die.

Like a flame, our human body is constantly changing. It only
seems as if it keeps more or less the same form.

Non-self doesn't mean absentmindedness. In the bodhisattva practice of the Great Vehicle, it's a matter of never being inattentive.

Even a camera can't capture reality if it's out of focus.

Practicing the Buddha way means kneading your approach to life.

Don't run around like a horse. Walk like an ox.

Even when just putting down a teacup, it makes a big difference if you simply let it fall or if you lower it carefully with your hand.

The basis of all actions is to follow through to the end. If your mind is absent even just for a moment, you're no different from a corpse.

It's all about finding the correct tension for your muscles and tendons. It's about becoming a person without gaps.

<hr>

"What image do I project to the eyes of humanity?"

"How do I look in other people's eyes?"

This question as well has to be studied with body and mind. How do I appear in a rich man's eyes? Or in a poor man's eyes? How does a Westerner see me? How does a Marxist see me? Who am I in the eyes of a prime minister?

You've got to have something about you that doesn't lose its luster, no matter where it's seen from.

<hr>

If you don't watch out, you'll become a superfluous Buddhist.

<hr>

What's the buddha-dharma about? It's about having every aspect of your daily life pulled by Buddha.

<hr>

It isn't enough to hit the bullseye once. Last's years perfect marks are useless. You've got to hit the bullseye right now.

Just eat your rice gruel. In this "just doing" there is neither high nor low, neither clever nor dumb, neither illusion nor satori.

This "just doing" is the essence of the Buddha way, but it's precisely this "just doing" that nobody in the world understands.

Everybody suffers from mixed-up views on life. That's why, in order to save humanity, it's essential to rethink new views on life from the bottom up, building on an absolutely solid foundation. To see life from this solid foundation means seeing it with the wisdom of Buddha.

EPILOGUE

To you who are still dissatisfied with your zazen.

by Kōshō Uchiyama

Dōgen Zenji's practice of shikantaza is exactly what my late teacher Kōdō Sawaki Rōshi called "the zazen of just sitting." So for me too, true zazen naturally means shikantaza—just sitting. That is to say that we do not practice zazen to have satori experiences, to solve a lot of kōans or receive a transmission certificate. Zazen just means to sit.

On the other hand, it is a fact that even among the practitioners of the Japanese Sōtō School, which goes back to its founder Dōgen Zenji, many have had doubts about this zazen. To make their point, they quote passages like these: "I have not visited many Zen monasteries. I simply, with my master Tendo, quietly verified that the eyes are horizontal and the nose is vertical. I cannot be misled by anyone anymore. I have returned home empty-handed."—Eihei Kōroku

"I travelled in Sung China and visited Zen masters in all parts of the country, studying the five houses of Zen. Finally, I met my master Nyojō on Taihaku peak, and the great matter of lifelong practice became clear. The great task of a lifetime of practice came to an end." —*Shōbōgenzō Bendōwa*

That's why they say, "Didn't even Dōgen Zenji say that he realized that the eyes are horizontal and the nose vertical, and that the great matter of lifelong practice became clear? What sense could there be when an ordinary person without a trace of satori just sits?"

I remember well carrying around such doubts myself—and I wasn't the only one. A significant number of the Zen practitioners who flocked around Sawaki Rōshi abandoned the zazen of just sitting in order to try out *kenshō* Zen or *kōan* Zen. So, I understand this doubt well.

We must know that Sawaki Rōshi had a Zen master's character, just as you might imagine it. He was also so charismatic that many, as soon as they first met him, were attracted to him like iron shavings to a magnet. So, when Rōshi said, "Zazen is good for absolutely nothing" (this was Sawaki Rōshi's expression for the zazen which is beyond gain and beyond satori), then they thought he was just saying that. They thought that their zazen practice would at some point actually be good for something or another. I think that goes for many who practiced with Sawaki Rōshi.

Perhaps those who lived outside and who just came to the temple for zazen or for a sesshin from time to time might not have had these doubts. But those who resolved to give up their former life to become monks and practice the day-to-day, intensive zazen life in the sangha around Sawaki Rōshi, these people sooner or later began to doubt *shikantaza*.

The reason for this is that, no matter how much you sit, you are never fully satisfied with your zazen. "Not fully satisfied" means that it does not feel the way your stomach does after a big meal. So many young people who had dedicated themselves, body and soul, to the practice of zazen began at some point to wonder if they weren't wasting their youth with this zazen that does not fill them up at all. Many finally left, saying: "Aren't even the older disciples, who have already been practicing this zazen for years, at bottom just ordinary people? I need satori!"

This is why many people gave up practicing. This doubt brought me almost to the breaking point as well, yet in the end I followed Sawaki Rōshi for twenty-four years until his death. So, I do understand those who entertain this doubt, but I have also finally understood the meaning of the *shikanta-za* of which Dōgen Zenji and Sawaki Rōshi speak. That is why I would now like to try to play the role of a sort of interpreter between the two standpoints.

When I say "interpreter," that doesn't mean only that many Zen practitioners don't understand the words of Dōgen Zenji or Sawaki Rōshi. I also mean that although Dōgen Zenji and Sawaki Rōshi *do* understand the deep doubts and problems of those who try to practice *shikantaza*, their words don't always reach far enough to truly soothe the root of our doubts and problems. That is why I permit myself to attempt here to present and comment on the following words of Dōgen Zenji and Sawaki Rōshi in my own way.

What does that mean in practice? Let's take for example the passage from Dōgen Zenji's *Eihei Kōroku*: "I simply, with my master Tendō Nyojō, quietly verified that the eyes are horizontal and the nose is vertical. From now on, I cannot be misled by anyone. I have returned home emptyhanded."

How would it be to read it like this: "Taking this breath at this moment, I verify that I am alive."

The reason why I can interpret it like this is because I don't read the *Shōbōgenzō* as a Buddhist scholar who is only concerned with bringing order to the labyrinth of Chinese characters. Nor do I read it as a sectarian to whom every single word is so holy that he puts it on a pedestal, like a tin of canned food that will never be opened, and throws himself to the ground before it. Instead, I read it with the eyes of a person who seeks the way, who is concerned with getting to the bottom of an entirely new way of life. I believe that is exactly what is meant by "seeing the mind in light of the ancient teachings" or "studying the Buddha way means studying the self."

If we read this passage from Dōgen Zenji as an expression of our own, entirely new life, we will not get stuck in a flat and static interpretation. Instead we will realize that "the eyes are horizontal, the nose is vertical" is an expression of this fresh life we are living, breathing this breath in this moment. When we read like this, we see that Dōgen Zenji isn't talking about some mystical state you might experience during zazen once you get "satori." He is talking about the most obvious fact— this life right here.

That is why it is also written at the beginning of Dōgen's *Fukanzazengi* (*A Universal Recommendation for Zazen*), "The way is omnipresent and complete. How can we distinguish practice from certification? The truth reveals itself by itself in every place, why make a special effort to grasp it?"

In the same spirit, what does the following passage mean? "A difference, even the breadth of a hair, separates heaven from Earth. If you make a distinction between favorable and unfavorable conditions, your mind will be lost in confusion."

Life in this moment is fresh, raw and new. But when we think about this essential fact as an idea in our heads, we get stuck, wondering about what we can understand and what we can force into our categories. When we think about the freshness of life, it isn't fresh anymore, it isn't alive. Freshness of life means opening the hand of thought. Only when we do so can life be fresh. Zazen is this opening this hand of thought. It is the posture of letting go.

Now I have to say a word about the actual practice of shikantaza. Sitting in zazen does not mean that we do not have any thoughts. All kinds of thoughts arise. Yet when you follow these thoughts, it can't be called zazen anymore. You are simply thinking in the posture of zazen. So, you have to realize that right now you are practicing zazen and it is not the time for thinking. This is correcting your attitude, correcting your posture, letting the thoughts go and returning to zazen. This is called "awakening from distraction and confusion."

Another time you might be tired. Then you have to remind yourself that you are practicing zazen right now, and it is not the time for sleeping. This is correcting your attitude, correcting your posture, really opening the eyes and returning to zazen. This is called "awakening from dullness and fatigue."

Zazen means awakening from distraction and confusion and from dullness and fatigue, awakening to zazen billions of times. The zazen of living out this fresh and raw life means awakening the mind, certifying through practice billions of times. This is *shikantaza*.

It's said that Dōgen Zenji achieved satori through dropping off body and mind, but what is this dropping off body and mind really? In his *Hōkyōki* we read, "The abbot said: 'The practice of zazen means dropping off body and mind. That means shikantaza—not burning incense, doing prostrations, nenbutsu, repentance or sutra reading.' I bowed and asked, 'What is dropping off body and mind?' The abbot answered, 'Dropping off body and mind is zazen. If you simply practice zazen, at that moment you are freed from the five desires and the five obstructions disappear.'"[22]

So, dropping off body and mind means opening the hand of thought and returning to zazen a billion times. Dropping off body and mind is not some sort of special mysterious experience.

Only this sort of zazen actualizes the entire, unsurpassable buddha-dharma. It is also called the "main gate to the buddha-dharma" (*Bendōwa*). I would like to compare our life to sitting behind the wheel of an automobile. When we drive,

---

[22] The five desires are the desires for the objects of the five sense objects; the five obstructions are greed, anger, indolence, agitation and doubt.

it is dangerous to fall asleep at the wheel or to drive drunk. It is also risky to think about other things while driving, or to be nervous and tense. That goes as well for sitting behind the wheel of our life. The fundamental approach to driving our life has to consist in waking up from the haze of sleepiness and drunkenness and from the distractions of thinking and nervousness.

Zazen means actually putting these basics of life into practice. That is why it can be called "seeing the whole of the buddha-dharma" or "the main gate of the buddha-dharma." That is also the reason why Dōgen Zenji wrote *Fukanzazengi*, in which he clarifies the practice of zazen.

"The body and mind of the Buddha way is grasses and trees, stones and tiles, wind and rain, fire and water. Observing this and recognizing everything as the Buddha way is what is meant by awakening bodhi-mind. Take hold of emptiness and use it to build pagodas and buddhas. Scoop out the water of the valley and use it to build buddhas and pagodas. That is what it means to arouse the awakened mind of unsurpassable, complete wisdom, and what it means to repeat this one single awakening billions of times. This is practicing realization." (*Shōbōgenzō Hotsumujōshin*).

It would be a big mistake to interpret this as a mere warning for all not-yet-awakened Zen practitioners to not neglect their practice. The billion-fold awakening of awakened mind does not mean anything more than the living breath of vigorous life.

Some people begin with the practice of shikantaza and then give it up quickly because it does not give them that feeling of fullness or because it bores them. They do so because they only understand this awakening a billion times in their heads. That's why they think, "Oh no! I have to awaken the mind a billion times? What I need is satori! If I hurry up and get one big satori, I can wrap up this billion-times business in a single stroke!"

It is exactly as if we were told as babies, "From now on you will have to breathe, your whole life long, this very breath, again and again, every single moment. You will breathe in and breathe out billions of times." What baby would say, "Oh no! I've got to find some way to take care of these billion breaths once and for all, with one really big breath!"

Even if we tried, we would not succeed.

That is why it continues in *Hotsumujōshin* further: "Some people believe that practice is indeed endless but awakening happens only once and that afterwards there is no awakening of the mind. Such a person does not hear the buddha-dharma, does not know the buddha-dharma and has never met the buddha-dharma."

People who try to get one big satori do not accept that they must live their life with all of its freshness and vigor. Even in strictly biological terms, we can only live by taking this breath in this moment. Living means breathing this breath right now. When it is a matter of living this fresh life, it is of course not enough to simply think about your life in your head. Instead, we have got to accept it as the vigorous life that it is. Only like this will we discover an attitude and posture which is fresh and vigorous.

That is what is meant by, "The great matter of lifelong practice has now come to an end." At the same time this is where the real practice of *shikantaza* begins. This is called "the unity of practice and realization" or "practice on the basis of realization."

That is why Sawaki Rōshi always repeated, "Satori has no beginning. Practice has no end!"

ABOUT THE AUTHOR & TRANSLATORS

Kōdō Sawaki (1880–1965) is widely considered to be one of the greatest Zen masters of the 20th century. Raised in exceedingly difficult conditions, he ran away at the age of sixteen to become a monk and spent years practicing with a wide range of masters. Later in life as well, though holding positions as a professor and abbot, he continued traveling throughout Japan to teach, earning the nickname, "Homeless Kōdō."

Sawaki is known for his direct, down-to-earth approach and his rigorous emphasis on zazen (*shikantaza*, or "just sitting"). He insists that Zen is not about self-improvement or spiritual attainment but is "good for nothing." After his passing, his teachings have continued through his disciples (notably Kosho Uchiyama and Taisen Deshimaru) and their successors.

Muhō Nölke (translator), born in 1968 in Berlin, was introduced to zazen as a high school student. In 1993, after graduating from university, he was ordained as a Sōtō Zen monk at the monastery Antai-ji. After obtaining the dharma transmission, he decided to live as a homeless monk in a park in Osaka, where he led a zazen group in 2001. In Feb. 2002, at the sudden death of his teacher, he was called back to Antai-ji. He succeeded his teacher as the ninth abbot, until his retirement in 2020. He teaches and lives in Osaka and has published many books and translations in both Japanese and German.

Reihō Jesse Haasch (translator) was born in Wisconsin in 1973. He followed a "path of books" until 1990 when he found a book describing the posture of zazen, which changed everything. In 1993 he met Robert Livingston (a disciple of Taisen Deshimaru) and was ordained a monk. In 1998 he moved to Switzerland and became a disciple of Michel Bovay until Bovay's death in 2009. Reihō moved to Japan and became a disciple of Hōkan Saitō Rōshi from whom he received the dharma transmission in 2015. He practices at Kōtaiji Monastery in Nagasaki, assists his teacher there and leads retreats and workshops in Europe.

ABOUT HOHM PRESS

HOHM PRESS is committed to publishing books that provide readers with alternatives to the materialistic values of the current culture, and promote self-awareness, the recognition of interdependence, and compassion. Our subject areas include parenting, transpersonal psychology, religious studies, women's studies, the arts and poetry.

Contact Information: Hohm Press, PO Box 4410, Chino Valley, Arizona, 86323, USA; 800-381-2700, or 928-636-3331; email: publisher@hohmpress.com

Visit our website at www.hohmpress.com